Contents

Preface

To the general reader

Although the *Access to History* series has been designed with the needs of students studying the subject at higher examination levels very much in mind, it also has a great deal to offer the general reader. The main body of the text (i.e. ignoring the Study Guides at the ends of chapters) forms a readable and yet stimulating survey of a coherent topic as studied by historians. However, each author's aim has not merely been to provide a clear explanation of what happened in the past (to interest and inform): it has also been assumed that most readers wish to be stimulated into thinking further about the topic and to form opinions of their own about the significance of the events that are described and discussed (to be challenged). Thus, although no prior knowledge of the topic is expected on the reader's part, she or he is treated as an intelligent and thinking person throughout. The author tends to share ideas and possibilities with the reader, rather than passing on numbers of so-called 'historical truths'.

To the student reader

Although advantage has been taken of the publication of a second edition to ensure the results of recent research are reflected in the text, the main alteration from the first edition is the inclusion of new features, and the modification of existing ones, aimed at assisting you in your study of the topic at AS level, A level and Higher. Two features are designed to assist you during your first reading of a chapter. The *Points to Consider* section following each chapter title is intended to focus your attention on the main theme(s) of the chapter, and the issues box following most section headings alerts you to the question or questions to be dealt with in the section. The *Working on . . .* section at the end of each chapter suggests ways of gaining maximum benefit from the chapter.

There are many ways in which the series can be used by students studying History at a higher level. It will, therefore, be worthwhile thinking about your own study strategy before you start your work on this book. Obviously, your strategy will vary depending on the aim you have in mind, and the time for study that is available to you.

If, for example, you want to acquire a general overview of the topic in the shortest possible time, the following approach will probably be the most effective:

1. Read chapter 1. As you do so, keep in mind the issues raised in the *Points to Consider* section.
2. Read the *Points to Consider* section at the beginning of chapter 2 and decide whether it is necessary for you to read this chapter.

3. If it is, read the chapter, stopping at each heading or sub-heading to note down the main points that have been made. Often, the best way of doing this is to answer the question(s) posed in the Issues boxes.

4. Repeat stage 2 (and stage 3 where appropriate) for all the other chapters.

If, however, your aim is to gain a thorough grasp of the topic, taking however much time is necessary to do so, you may benefit from carrying out the same procedure with each chapter, as follows:

1. Read the chapter as fast as you can, and preferably at one sitting. As you do this, bear in mind any advice given in the *Points to Consider* section.

2. Study the flow diagram at the end of the chapter, ensuring that you understand the general 'shape' of what you have just read.

3. Read the *Working on...* section and decide what further work you need to do on the chapter. In particularly important sections of the book, this is likely to involve reading the chapter a second time and stopping at each heading and sub-heading to think about (and probably to write a summary of) what you have just read.

4. Attempt the *Source-based questions* section. It will sometimes be sufficient to think through your answers, but additional understanding will often be gained by forcing yourself to write them down.

When you have finished the main chapters of the book, study the 'Further Reading' section and decide what additional reading (if any) you will do on the topic.

This book has been designed to help make your studies both enjoyable and successful. If you can think of ways in which this could have been done more effectively, please contact us. In the meantime, we hope that you will gain greatly from your study of History.

Keith Randell

1 The Third Reich – An Introduction

POINTS TO CONSIDER

This chapter serves as a brief introduction to the study of the Third Reich. Above all, your aim during your first reading should be to identify as many as possible of the 'big issues' and problems.

KEY DATES

1871 Unification of Germany in wake of Franco-Prussian War.
1888 Accession of Kaiser Wilhelm II.
1918 Surrender of Germany in First World War. Abdication of Kaiser and declaration of republic.
1933 Hitler appointed Chancellor and establishment of Nazi dictatorship.
1939 Outbreak of Second World War.
1945 German surrender; division of Germany by Allies.
1949 Creation of Federal Republic of Germany (West Germany) and German Democratic Republic (East Germany).
1990 Reunification of Germany after fall of Berlin Wall in 1989.

1　Whatever one may think of his [Hitler's] methods – and they are certainly not those of a parliamentary country – there can be no doubt that he has achieved a marvellous transformation in the spirit of the people, in their attitude towards each other, and in their social and economic
5　outlook ... As to his popularity, especially among the youth of Germany, there can be no manner of doubt. The old trust him; the young idolise him. It is not the admiration accorded to a popular leader. It is the worship of a national hero who has saved his country from utter despondency and degradation ... He is the George Washington
10　of Germany.[1]

These words were written in 1937, not by a Nazi, not even by a Nazi sympathiser, but by a Welshman, a Liberal and a former British prime minister – David Lloyd George. Of course, numerous contemporary assessments of Hitler's Germany were published and they ranged widely from fulsome praise to outraged contempt. Yet, since 1945 when the grim reality of Nazism had become apparent, eulogies for the Third Reich have essentially remained the preserve of politically motivated right-wing extremists. Indeed, there is probably no other regime in history which has been so universally condemned by serious academic scholarship. However, despite such unanimity, there is certainly no modern-day consensus when it comes to explaining Nazism – quite the reverse. The Third Reich has become one of the most controversial fields of historical study, for it has not only generated the usual kinds of dispute over points of analysis and interpretation: it has also raised issues of morality and philosophy which have brought into question the very nature of the historian's craft.

1 The Historical Issues

KEY ISSUE What are the major areas of historical controversy among historians of the Third Reich?

As with so many of history's great controversies, it is the questions of causation and definition which have prompted the most vigorous debate. How and why were the Nazis able to gain power and why was it possible to create and maintain a regime of such brutality? What exactly was Nazism and what did it represent?

At the very centre of all these questions stands the figure of Hitler himself. For some, the 'Hitler factor' provides reassuring proof that history unfolds as the result of the power, influence and actions of the individual. In this sense, Hitler can be seen as one of the 'great men' of history (albeit in the evil category), as a leader, comparable to Julius Caesar or Napoleon Bonaparte, who created a powerful political movement, directed his nation's affairs according to his will and then led the world into one of the most destructive military conflicts ever. Many eminent historians maintain the basic validity of a Hitler-centred interpretation of the Third Reich, and they are described as belonging to the 'intentionalist' school. Cynics might argue that the 'intentionalist' interpretation is rather convenient, since it allows much of the blame for the crimes of Nazism to be directed towards a dead Führer. However, there is plenty of historical research to support the idea that the personal role of Hitler has been greatly over-emphasised. Historians of the 'structuralist' school have played down the significance of Hitler and his intentions and have instead focused their attention on the structure of the Third Reich in its broadest sense. In particular, they have examined the apparatus of Party and state in order to identify the political complexities of the regime and its decision-making processes. For the student approaching the subject for the first time it is, of course, impossible to ignore the position of Hitler. However, it is vitally important to avoid being drawn automatically into a Hitler-centred analysis. His power and influence must be assessed: they must not be automatically assumed.

Although this book deals almost exclusively with Germany, it should not be forgotten that the Third Reich coincided with a number of other regimes which have been labelled 'fascist' and/or 'totalitarian'. This led some historians (and more particularly political scientists) to portray Nazism as the German example of a common type of mid-twentieth-century political movement. Left-wing analysts, for example, have traditionally favoured 'generic' interpretations of fascism, which have emphasised the vital importance of economic forces and the class alignments within capitalist societies to explain the emergence of fascist systems of government. However, the explanation of Nazism as merely a variety of fascism carries with it many far-reaching implications. In particular, it raises the possibility that Nazism was not a historical phenomenon which resulted from a unique set of circumstances and that its roots were not necessarily Germanic, let alone purely Hitlerian. Likewise, the application of the term 'totalitarian' to the Third Reich has been favoured by more liberal historians who have sought to underline the similarities between left- and right-wing one-party states. According to such a view, Nazism could not only be compared to contemporary regimes such as that of Mussolini's Italy, Franco's Spain and Stalin's Russia, but also to the post-war people's republics of eastern Europe. Clearly, the Third Reich should not be studied in isolation and so it is important to compare and contrast the history of Germany with developments in Italy, Spain and the USSR. However, one must avoid the temptation of forcing the Third Reich to conform to certain predetermined political models. The European context must be borne in mind, whilst allowing for the particular circumstances which permitted the development of National Socialism in Germany.

Those historians who have not wished to explore the implications of such parallels have tended to emphasise Nazi racial and foreign policy as its most distinguishing features of uniqueness. According to such a view, the importance placed by the Nazis on their racial ideology, which in turn provided the justification for their expansionist programme of conquest and domination, sets it apart from all other regimes. And, certainly, the grandiose nature of Nazi imperial ambitions, together with the brutal and clinical implementation of the racial 'new order', have been vital factors in making the Third Reich the focus of such attention. The attempted genocide of the Jews, the resettlement and murder of millions of other 'inferior' people, and the bloodshed wrought on Germany's own people, are happenings which not only require rational historical analysis, but also arouse questions about the nature of mankind and of morality.

A further controversial issue relating to the Third Reich involves an assessment of the extent of its 'revolutionary' character. This has been a point of heated debate amongst historians for many years. For some, Nazism is viewed as an abhorrent aberration, which clearly marked a fundamental change of direction in Germany's evolutionary path. For others, it came to represent the natural culmination of developments within Germany since the middle of the nineteenth century. This question of continuity and change is central to any understanding, explanation and definition of the Third Reich. However, in order to appreciate its subtleties, it is necessary to place the Third Reich in the context of recent German history.

2 The Historical Context

> **KEY ISSUES** What are the key features in German history between 1871 and 1990? What should be understood by the concepts of continuity and change in this context?

In 1871, in the wake of the Franco-Prussian War, the German Empire was proclaimed. For the first time in their history the states of Germany had been formally unified. Seventy-four years later, amidst the ruins of its major cities, Hitler's Third Reich surrendered to the Allies, thus ushering in the division of Germany and the creation of two separate German states which lasted until 1990.

From its inception, the German Empire, or *Kaiserreich*, bore the stamp both of its creator, Bismarck, and of the circumstances of its creation. Its federal constitution, whilst making concessions to provincial feelings, allowed for the domination of Prussia, the strongest of all the federal states. Moreover, the King of Prussia was also Kaiser (Emperor) of Germany and his powers were immense: he alone chose the imperial chancellor; he ultimately decided matters of foreign policy; and he was supreme commander of the combined armed forces of the Empire. Thus, despite the existence of an imperial parliament, the Reichstag, and a federal council, there was no disguising the fact that effective power lay with the Kaiser and his chosen chancellor. Whilst Wilhelm I (1871–88) and Chancellor Bismarck worked in tandem the system was able to work moderately well. But the coming to power of Wilhelm II (1888–1918) ushered in a new and more uncertain era, which highlighted a number of inherent weaknesses in the political arrangements of the Empire. Wilhelm II's own personal failings of character made him unsuited to the direction of affairs of state. This meant that, despite the lofty ideals and the great plans, there was no real consistency in policy-making. Constitutional problems were further exacerbated by developments in the German economy and society. Industrialisation had made Germany the strongest economy on the continent, but it had also wrought fundamental changes in the relative strength and importance of the various classes in society. The rise of an entrepreneurial middle class and a large working class was clearly a threat to the established social order. By 1914 the Social Democrats, as the political party representing the working classes, had become by far the largest parliamentary party and yet, the powers of the Reichstag remained strictly limited by the terms of the constitutional arrangements made in 1871. As a result, on the eve of the First World War, Germany was still an authoritarian monarchy, bolstered by a number of traditional conservative interest groups, or elites. The most significant of these were the Army, the bureaucracy and the *Junkers* (the large landowners).

Whether Germany could have evolved peacefully into some kind of constitutional democracy remains open to debate. However, there can be little doubt that the strains and resentments generated by total war during 1914–18 not only caused the demise of the *Kaiserreich* in the revolution at the end of 1918, but also contributed decisively to the political developments of the next fifteen years.

The Weimar Republic, which replaced the *Kaiserreich*, was flawed from the moment of its birth. It was the product of military defeat and the social distress caused by war and, in this sense, its creation was a 'knee-jerk' reaction to a crisis, rather than the result of a genuine desire for fundamental change. Moreover, it meant that subsequently democratic parties were associated with national humiliation, which gave currency to the myth of the 'stab in the back' – the idea that the politicians had betrayed the country by surrendering when the Army could still have won the war. This situation was in turn greatly exacerbated by the imposition on Germany of the extremely harsh Treaty of Versailles, since the new republic was saddled with the responsibility of accepting what to most Germans was unacceptable. Even the new constitution, drawn up with such careful consideration, ended up as a series of compromises between the forces of revolution and reaction, which allowed for the survival of the traditional vested interests while also advancing sophisticated democratic procedures and principles. Unfortunately for the republic, the new institutions did not always show the expected loyalty to the constitution, nor sufficient commitment to the values of an open, pluralist democracy.

Nor was a sizeable part of the population supportive of the political principles upon which Weimar was based. In the Reichstag election in June 1920 35 per cent of the electorate supported non-democratic parties of either the extreme left or the extreme right. From 1920 Weimar 'democracy' veered between weak, short-lived cabinets and authoritarian government upheld by means of the president's emergency powers. The republic managed to overcome the Kapp *Putsch* of 1920 (an attempted *coup* by Army officers supported by conservative nationalists). It even survived the much greater crises of 1923 – the French occupation of the Ruhr and the 'Great Inflation'. However, the implications of such episodes for the long-term survival of democracy were profound: the loyalty of the Army to the republic was uncertain; public confidence had been hit hard by the inflation; the German economy was in a weakened state and very much at the mercy of international forces; and powerful militaristic and nationalist groups had made clear their intention to destroy the regime.

Even in the period of so-called prosperity and stability from 1924 to 1929 it was impossible to disguise the fundamental political weakness. Coalition governments (often without a majority in the Reichstag) came and went with alarming frequency, and were often only created after considerable intrigue and compromise. Field Marshal Hindenburg, who had limited sympathy for the regime, was elected President in 1925 – a post he was not prepared to accept until he had gained the permission of the ex-Kaiser!

When the depression which started in 1929 finally brought economic ruin to Weimar Germany it created an environment in which anti-republican forces could flourish. Thus, in the years 1930–3, as the number of voters sympathetic to democracy declined, so did the chance of saving the young republic. Germany was already a semi-dictatorship from September 1930. By 1932 only 43 per cent of the electorate voted in the July Reichstag elections for pro-republican parties. In the light of this evidence, it is difficult to escape the conclusion that Weimar-style democracy was unlikely to survive. This, of course, is not to argue that the establishment of the Nazi regime in 1933 was a natural consequence – merely that anti-democratic forces of some type were likely to gain power.

Naturally, one would expect to find aspects of both continuity and change in the history of Germany between 1871 and 1945. The crucial historical task is to decide where the overall balance between the two lies. So, although the aim of this book is to explore some of the most significant issues concerning National Socialism, it is important to be aware of the historical background. In particular, the following themes need to be seen within this broader sweep of German history: the nature of the political structure and the part played by the key interest groups; the importance attached to certain political and social attitudes, especially racism, anti-democracy and anti-socialism; and, finally, the vital issue of Germany's position in the international arena. In this way, it should be possible to come to an informed provisional judgement about whether the Third Reich represents the final phase in a continuity based upon the military-state structure founded in 1871, or whether it marks a revolutionary break with the traditions of Germany's previous history.

3 The Problems of Historical Interpretation

> **KEY ISSUE** Why does the Third Reich create particular problems of historical interpretation?

In November 1989 the Berlin Wall, the symbol of post-war division, came down and one year later Germany once again became a unified state. Such dramatic developments underlined the truth behind the maxim that history is always a product of the time in which it is written. The reunification of Germany had seemed an impossibility only months previously. Until then historians had naturally based their analyses from the perspective of a clearly divided Germany, which seemed to suggest that the period of unity from 1871 to 1945 was merely a 'blip' in the long-term tradition of division and disunity. But, since the events of 1989–90, a reunited Germany at the heart of the continent has not only posed key questions for Germany's (and Europe's) political leaders, it has also prompted a welter of discussion and interpretation about Germany's long-term historical development.

Our historical perspective is therefore rarely static for very long. This is particularly the case with the Third Reich, which has developed into one of the great historiographical debates of the last 50 years. The steady stream of new books on the subject shows no sign of drying up. This, to some extent, reflects the huge range of archive material available on this topic – a source-base which continues to grow as more and more material is released by the authorities in areas which were previously under Soviet control. The sheer volume of evidence clearly presents the historian of the Third Reich with very different problems to those faced by those who are researching a much earlier period of German history. Even so, historians are rarely satisfied with the available evidence. They always want more. And so the knowledge that a wealth of material was destroyed – either deliberately or as a result of the war – is a cause of considerable frustration. The revelation of the so-called 'Hitler diaries' (later shown to be fakes) in the 1980s created such excitement amongst academic historians mainly because it raised the possibility of explaining the nature of Nazi government, about which great uncertainty still remains because of the partial and conflicting nature of the surviving evidence.

However, the controversies surrounding the Third Reich go much deeper than differences over the interpretation of evidence, as was recently revealed by the state of 'open warfare' which developed within Germany's academic community. The Third Reich became the focus of a vitriolic debate, soon dubbed the *Historikerstreit* (historians' dispute), although its waves reverberated well beyond university walls. At the heart of this dispute lay the fundamental problems facing any student of the Third Reich. How do you interpret rationally and objectively a subject clouded by the horrors of the Holocaust? Secondly, is it possible to 'historicise' (consider in a truly historical fashion) the Third Reich as a normal period of history? And finally, specifically for the German student, there remains the problem of trying to come to terms with the Nazi past as part of one's own national identity.

Almost inevitably, as the Third Reich recedes into the past, the increased time-gap creates a certain detachment which allows for greater objectivity. Yet, even after so many years, some people would still argue that the subject of Nazism is too loaded with political and moral overtones for the normal standards of historical scholarship to apply. Therein, perhaps, lies an explanation of why the subject continues to be the focus of such interest for the layman and the historian. The Third Reich is a particularly daunting intellectual challenge, but it is one which cannot be ignored.

Reference

1   D.L. George in the *Daily Express*, 17 November 1936

Summary Diagram
Introduction

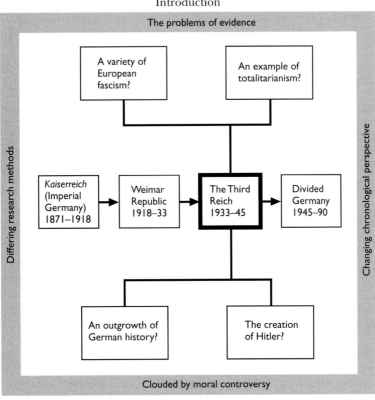

Working on Chapter 1

If you have already studied pre-Nazi German history, the second section of this chapter should present few problems. Indeed, it would probably be better to look back on your previous notes and then to jot down anything which seems unfamiliar. However, if modern German history is a new historical topic, then you will have to re-read this section carefully and try to understand as much as you can. Alternatively, you could look at the companion volume in this series, *From Bismarck to Hitler*. Sections 1 and 3 are more demanding, and many students will probably find some of the ideas difficult to grasp. If you can write brief answers to each of the questions posed in the issues boxes, your mind will at least have started to think about some of the most important points.

2 Hitler and the Nazi Party – the Road to Power

From the very start, Hitler's appointment as Chancellor on 30 January 1933 prompted extensive analysis. Nowadays, as then, the debate about Hitler's rise to power concentrates on the historical issue of causation. In particular, it prompts two key questions, which although intimately linked, are different: 'Why did Weimar democracy fail?' and 'Why did the Nazis, and not some other political group, take power?' It is the latter question which is the real focus of this chapter, although clearly any explanation of the Nazi take-over has to bear in mind the weaknesses and failings of the Weimar Republic. As you read it for the first time, try to be aware of the wide range of contributory factors which are being referred to: the Hitler factor; the circumstances of the time; the weaknesses of the opposition.

KEY DATES

1920	Feb	NSDAP 25-point Party programme drawn up.
1923	8 Nov	Beer Hall *putsch* in Munich: disastrous fiasco.
1924		Hitler in Landsberg prison. *Mein Kampf* written.
1925	27 Feb	NSDAP refounded.
1926	Feb	Bamberg conference: Hitler's leadership of the Party re-established.
1929	Oct	Death of Gustav Stresemann and Wall Street Crash.
1930	Mar	Collapse of Müller's coalition government. Appointment of Brüning as Chancellor.
	Sept	Reichstag election: Nazis emerged as second largest party (107 seats).
1932	Apr	Re-election of Hindenburg as President.
	May	Resignation of Brüning. Papen became Chancellor.
	July	Reichstag election: Nazis by far the largest party (230 seats).
	Dec	Resignation of Papen. Appointment of Schleicher as Chancellor.
1933	30 Jan	Hitler appointed Chancellor.

1 Hitler's Early Years

> **KEY ISSUES** How did Hitler become involved in politics? What were his main ideas?

There was little in the background of Adolf Hitler (1889–1945) to suggest that he would become a powerful political figure. Hitler was born at Braunau-am-Inn in 1889 in what was then the Austro-Hungarian Empire. He failed to impress at school, and after the death of his parents he moved to Vienna in 1907. There he applied unsuccessfully for a place as a student at the Academy of Fine Arts. For the next six years he led an aimless and unhappy existence in the poorer districts of the city. It was not until he joined the Bavarian Regiment on the outbreak of war in 1914 that he found a real purpose in life. He served bravely throughout the war, and was awarded the Iron Cross First Class. When the war ended he was in hospital recovering from a British gas attack. By the time he had returned to Bavaria in early 1919 he had already framed in his mind the core of what was to become National Socialism: a fervent German nationalism; a hatred of democracy and socialism; and a racially inspired view of society which exhibited itself most obviously in a rabid anti-Semitism and a veneration of the German *Volk* as the master race.

Such a mixture of ideas in a man whose personal life was also much of a mystery – he had no close family and few real friends – has excited 'psycho-historians' to extraordinary speculation. Did his anti-Semitism originate from contracting syphilis from a Jewish prostitute? Could his authoritarian disposition be explained by his upbringing at the hands of an old and repressive father? Such psychological diagnoses – and there are many – may interest the student, but the supporting evidence for such explanations is at best flimsy. As a result, the conclusions reached are highly speculative and do not really help to explain the key question of how and why Hitler became such an influential political force.

It was because of his entrenched right-wing attitudes that Hitler was employed in the politically charged atmosphere of 1919 as a kind of spy by the political department of the Army's Bavarian section. One of his investigations brought him into contact with the DAP (*Deutsche Arbeiterpartei* – German Workers' Party) which was not a movement of the revolutionary left, as Hitler had assumed on hearing its name, but one committed to nationalism, anti-Semitism and anti-capitalism. Hitler joined the tiny party and immediately became a member of its committee. His energy, oratory and propaganda skills soon made an impact on the small group, and it was Hitler who with the Party's founder, Anton Drexler, drew up the Party's 25-point programme in February 1920. At the same time it was agreed to change the Party's name to the NSDAP, the National Socialist German Workers' Party.

By mid-1921 it was clear Hitler was the driving-force behind the Party, although he still only held the post of propaganda chief. It was his powerful speeches which had impressed local audiences and had helped increase party membership to 3,300. He had encouraged the creation of the armed squads to protect Party meetings. It was his development of early propaganda techniques – the Nazi salute, the swastika, the uniforms – which had done so much to give the Party a clear and easily recognisable identity. Alarmed by Hitler's increasing

Extracts from the 25-point programme of the NSDAP
1 We demand the union of all Germans in a Greater Germany on the basis of the right of national self-determination.
2 We demand equality of rights for the German People in its dealings with other nations, and the revocation of the peace treaties of Versailles and Saint Germain.
3 We demand land and territory (colonies) to feed our people and to settle our surplus population.
4 Only members of the *Volk* (nation) may be citizens of the State. Only those of German blood, whatever their creed may be members of the nation. Accordingly no Jew may be a member of the nation.
7 We demand that the State shall make it its primary duty to provide a livelihood for its citizens. If it should prove impossible to feed the entire population, non-citizens must be deported from the Reich.
10 It must be the first duty of every citizen to perform physical or mental work. The activities of the individual must not clash with the general interest, but must proceed within the framework of the community and be for the general good.
11 We demand therefore the abolition of incomes unearned by work.
14 We demand profit-sharing in large industrial enterprises.
15 We demand the extensive development of insurance for old age.
18 We demand the ruthless prosecution of those whose activities are injurious to the common interest. Common criminals, usurers, profiteers must be punished with death, whatever their creed or race
22 We demand the abolition of the mercenary army and the formation of a people's army.
23 We demand legal warfare on deliberate political mendacity and its dissemination in the press.
(For an analysis of Nazi ideology see pages 12–15)

domination of the Party, Drexler and some other members of the committee tried to curtail his influence. In the ensuing power struggle Hitler soon mobilised support and at two meetings in July 1921 he won sufficient support to become chairman and Führer (leader) of the Party.

Having gained supreme control over the Party in Munich, Hitler aimed to subordinate the other 45 semi-autonomous branches to his leadership. To a large extent this was achieved within Bavaria in the years 1921–3, but it proved impossible with those groups further afield. This period also witnessed the staging of the first party rally and the development of the armed squads into an organised group – the SA (*Sturm Abteilung* – Stormtroopers).

2 The Beer-Hall *Putsch*, 1923

> **KEY ISSUES** Why did the Beer Hall *putsch* fail? How was failure
> turned to advantage?

The successful take-over of power by Mussolini in Italy in October
1922, combined with the developing internal crisis in Germany, convinced Hitler that the opportunity to seize power had arrived. But the
Nazis were far too weak on their own to stage any kind of political
take-over. It was the need for allies which led Hitler into negotiations
with the Bavarian State Government and the Bavarian section of the
Army during 1923.

The government of the State of Bavaria was led by the ultra-
conservative Gustav von Kahr, who blamed most of Germany's problems
on the socialist-dominated government in Berlin. Like Hitler, he wished
to destroy the republican regime, although his long-term aim was the
creation of an independent Bavaria. By October 1923 General von
Lossow, the Army's commander in Bavaria, had fallen under von Kahr's
spell and had even begun to disobey orders from the Defence Minister.

It was with these two men that Hitler plotted to 'March on Berlin'
in the style of Mussolini's *coup*. However, at the eleventh hour, von
Kahr and von Lossow, fearing failure, decided to abandon the plan.
Hitler was not so cautious and preferred to press on rather than lose
the opportunity. On 8 November, when von Kahr was addressing a
large audience in one of Munich's beer halls, Hitler and the Nazis
took control of the meeting and declared a 'national revolution'.
Drama soon turned into farce. Hitler had insufficient support from
the Army and police, and the attempted take-over of Munich was
easily crushed. Fourteen Nazis were killed and Hitler himself was
arrested on a charge of treason.

Despite the inglorious result, Hitler gained much political advantage from the episode. He won the respect of many other right-wing
nationalists for having had the courage to act and he turned his trial
into a propaganda success both for himself and for the Nazi cause.
Indeed his sentence of five years (the minimum stipulated by the
Weimar Constitution and actually reduced to ten months) seemed
like an act of encouragement on the part of the judiciary.

3 The Ideology of National Socialism

> **KEY ISSUE** What were the key features of Nazi ideology?

Nazism always emphasised the importance of action over thought.
However, whilst in Landsberg prison, Hitler dictated the first part of

Mein Kampf (*My Struggle*) which in the following years became the bible of National Socialism. Together with the 25-point programme of 1920, it provides the basic framework of Hitler's ideology and, by extension, of Nazism itself.

Hitler's ideas were built upon his concept of race. He believed that humanity consisted of a graduated hierarchy of races and that life was no more than 'the survival of the fittest'. He argued that Social Darwinism necessitated a struggle between races, just as animals fought for food and territory in the wild. Furthermore, he considered it vital to maintain racial purity, so that the strong would not be undermined by the blood of the weak.

It was a crude philosophy, which appears even more simplistic when Hitler's analysis of the races is considered. The *Herrenvolk* (master-race) was the Aryan race, made up of the peoples of Northern Europe and epitomised by the Germans. It was the task of the Aryan to remain pure and to subjugate the inferior races. At the lower end of his racial pyramid Hitler placed the Negroes, the Slavs, the Gypsies and, the particular focus of his hatred, the Jews. Hitler's anti-Semitism was violent and irrational. The Jew became the universal scapegoat for the Nazis, responsible for all the problems of Germany past and present. Hitler saw the Jewish community as a kind of cancer within the German body politic – a disease that had to be treated, as the following extract from *Mein Kampf* illustrates:

1 The adulteration of the blood and racial deterioration conditioned thereby are the only causes that account for the decline of ancient civilisations; for it is never by war that nations are ruined, but by the loss of their powers of resistance, which are exclusively a characteristic of
5 pure racial blood. In this world everything that is not of sound stock is like chaff. Every historical event in the world is nothing more nor less than a manifestation of the instinct of racial self-preservation, whether for weal or woe.

A number of points in the 1920 programme demanded socialist reforms, and for a long time there existed a faction within the Party which emphasised the anti-capitalist aspect of Nazism. Hitler accepted these points in the early years because he recognised their popular appeal, but he himself never showed any real commitment to such ideas, and they were to be dropped after he came to power. What Hitler did promote was the concept of the *Volksgemeinschaft* (people's community). This remained the vaguest element of the Nazi ideology, and is therefore difficult to define precisely. It was intended to overcome the old identities of class, religion and politics and to bring about a new collective national identity by people working together for the benefit of the nation and by the encouragement of 'German values'. Such a system could of course only benefit those who belonged to the German *Volk* and who willingly accepted the loss of individual freedoms in an authoritarian system.

In Hitler's opinion there was no realistic alternative to strong dictatorial government. Ever since his years in Vienna he had viewed parliamentary democracy as weak and ineffective. It went against the German historical traditions of militarism and absolutism, and furthermore it encouraged the development of an even greater evil, communism. More specifically, Hitler saw Weimar democracy as a betrayal. In his eyes, it was the democratic and socialist politicians of 1918, 'the November Criminals', who had stabbed the German Army in the back, by accepting the armistice and establishing the Republic. Since then Germany had lurched from crisis to crisis. In place of democracy Hitler envisaged the creation of an all-embracing one-party state that would be run on the leadership principle (*Führerprinzip*). Thus, the mass of individuals in society were to be subjugated for the common good, but the individual leader was to be elevated in order to rouse the nation into action, and to take the necessary decisions.

The final element in Nazi ideology was an aggressive nationalism, which developed out of the particular circumstances of Germany's recent history. The armistice of 1918 and the subsequent Treaty of Versailles had to be overturned, and the lost territories had to be restored to Germany. But Hitler's nationalism called for more than a mere restoration of the 1914 frontiers. It meant the creation of an empire (Reich) to include all those members of the German *Volk* who lived beyond the frontiers of the Kaiser's Germany: the Austrian Germans, the Sudeten Germans, the German communities along the Baltic coast, all were to be included within the borders of Germany. Yet, Hitler's nationalist aims did not end there. He dreamed of a Greater Germany, a superpower, capable of competing with the British Empire and the United States. Such an objective could be achieved only by territorial expansion on a grand scale. This was the basis of Hitler's demand for *Lebensraum* (living-space) for Germany. Only by the conquest of Poland, the Ukraine and Russia could Germany obtain the raw materials, cheap labour and food supplies so necessary for continental supremacy. The creation of his 'New Order' in eastern Europe also held one other great attraction: namely, it would involve the destruction of the USSR, the centre of world communism. As he argued in *Mein Kampf*:

1 The German people must be assured the territorial area which is necessary for it to exist on earth ... People of the same blood should be in the same Reich. The German people will have no right to engage in a colonial policy until they shall have brought all their children
5 together in one state. When the territory of the Reich embraces all the Germans and finds itself unable to assure them a livelihood, only then can the moral right arise, from the need of the people, to acquire foreign territory. The plough is then the sword; and the tears of war will produce the daily bread for the generations to come ... In the
10 future our people will not obtain territory, and therewith the means of

existence, as a favour from any other people, but will have to win it by the power of a triumphant sword. . . .

   The right to territory may become a duty when a great nation seems destined to go under unless its territory be extended. And this is par-
15 ticularly true when the nation in question is not some little group of negro people but the Germanic mother of all the life which has given cultural shape to the modern world. Germany will either become a World Power or will not continue to exist at all. . . . The future goal of our foreign policy ought to be an Eastern policy which will have in view
20 the acquisition of such territory as is necessary for our German people. To carry out this policy we need the force which the mortal enemy of our nation, France, now deprives us of.

To describe Hitler's thinking as an ideology is really to flatter it. It lacked coherence and was intellectually superficial and simplistic. It was not even a rational system of thought. It was merely a collection of ideas not very cleverly pieced together. Although the combination was unique, it was not in any positive sense original. Every aspect of Hitler's thinking was to be found in the nationalist and racist writings of the nineteenth century. His nationalism was an outgrowth of the fervour generated in Germany in the years between Prussia's struggle against Napoleon and the unification of 1871. His idea of an all-German Reich was a simple repetition of the demands for the 'Greater Germany' made by those German nationalists who criticised Bismarck's limited unification. Even the imperialism of *Lebensraum* had already found expression in the programme of 'Germanisation' supported by those writers who saw the German race as somehow superior. This growing veneration for the *Volk* had also gone hand-in-hand with the development of racist ideas, and in particular of anti-Semitism. Thus, even before Hitler and other leading Nazis were born, the core of what would become Nazism was already current in political circles. It was to be found in the cheap and vulgar pamphlets sold to the masses in the large cities; in the political programme of respectable pressure groups, such as the Pan-German League; within the corridors of Germany's great universities; and in the creative works of certain cultural figures such as the composer Richard Wagner. However, despite these links, one must avoid labelling Nazi ideology as the logical result of Germany's intellectual legacy. It is all too easy to search out those elements which prove the linkage theory whilst ignoring the host of other evidence which points to entirely different intellectual traditions – and there were many in the case of Germany. Moreover, it is well to remember that a number of countries, but especially Britain and France, also witnessed the propagation of very similar ideas at this time. In that sense nationalism and racism were an outgrowth of nineteenth-century European history. Nazi ideology may not have been original, but it should not therefore be assumed that it was an inevitable result of Germany's past.

4 The Creation of a Party Structure

> **KEY ISSUE** How was the Party reformed after 1925?

In Landsberg prison Hitler reflected on the failure of the 1923 *Putsch*. He concluded that an armed *coup* was no longer an appropriate tactic and that the only sure way to succeed was to work within the Weimar constitution and to gain power by legal means. Such a policy of legality would necessitate the creation of a party structure geared to gaining success at the ballot box.

However, when Hitler left prison in December 1924 the future looked bleak. The Party was in disarray: its leading members were split into factions and the membership was in decline. More significantly, the atmosphere of crisis which had prevailed in the early years of the republic had given way to a period of political and economic calm. The Party was officially refounded on 27 February 1925, but it was a party deeply divided in a number of ways. Not everyone agreed with the new policy of legality. Traditional regional hostilities, particularly between Catholic Bavaria and Protestant Prussia, continued to exist. Most importantly, policy differences had emerged between the nationalist and anti-capitalist wings of the Party. For over a year Hitler struggled with this internal friction, until eventually in February 1926, at a special Party conference in Bamberg, he mobilised sufficient support to re-establish his supremacy. The Nazi Party was to be run according to the *Führerprinzip* (leadership principle). There was to be no place for the discussion of differences.

The most significant development in the years before the Depression lay in the reorganisation of the Party structure. The whole of Germany was divided into regions (*Gaue*), which reflected the electoral geography of Weimar's system of proportional representation. The control of each region was placed in the hands of a *Gauleiter*, who then had the responsibility of creating district (*Kreis*) and branch (*Ort*) groups. In this way a vertical Party structure was created throughout Germany, which did not detract from Hitler's own position of authority as leader. At the same time a number of new Nazi organisations were founded: the SS, an elite body of black-shirted guards, sworn to absolute obedience to the Führer; the Hitler Youth, to attract the support of the young; and the Nazi Teachers' Association. The Party was taking shape and its membership was increasing: 27,000 in 1925, 49,000 in 1926, and 72,000 in 1927. Moreover, it had successfully taken over most of the other right-wing racist groups in Germany. Such progress, however, could not compensate for the disappointment of the election in May 1928, when the Party won only 2.6 per cent of the vote and a mere twelve seats in the Reichstag. It seemed as if the improvement in the Party's organisation and the policy of legality had failed to bring political success.

5 The Impact of the Great Depression

> **KEY ISSUE** How did the economic problems of the Great
> Depression create an environment of opportunity for the Nazis?

The problems facing the young Weimar Republic are such a vital feature of the years 1929–33 that they must be considered as an integral
factor in creating the situation in which Hitler and Nazism were to
gain political power. This is not to deny that Weimar was actually
already facing profound underlying pressures, but the death of
Gustav Stresemann, the only democratic politician of real stature, in
the very same month as the Wall Street Crash ushered in a major
world economic depression, precipitated an environment of crisis in
which the Nazis were able to thrive.

Germany was probably more susceptible to the consequences of
the USA's financial crash than any other country. Almost immediately
the American loans and investment dried up and this was soon followed by demands for the repayment of those loans which had been
advanced so willingly over the previous five years. At the same time,
the Crash precipitated a further decline in the prices of food and raw
materials, as industrialised nations reduced their imports. But the
knock-on effects of this action rebounded upon the more advanced
economies, since many primary producers could no longer afford to
import manufactured goods. World trade slumped as demand collapsed. In this situation German industry could no longer pay its way.
Unsupported by loans and with diminished export markets, prices
and wages fell whilst the number of bankruptcies increased. During
the winter of 1929–30 unemployment rose above 2 million. Only 12
months after the Crash, it had reached 3 million. By September 1932
it stood at 5.1 million. It peaked in early 1933, when 6.1 million
Germans were unemployed. Germany was faced with yet another
major economic and social crisis, only a few years after the trauma of
the 'Great Inflation'.

Economic statistics on their own can provide only a limited understanding of an event like the Depression. The unemployment figures,
for example, do not take into account those who never registered.
Nor do they recognise the extent of short-time working throughout
German industry. Above all, statistics fail to convey the extent of the
human consequences of this disaster. For the Depression in Germany
was all pervasive; few families escaped its detrimental effects. Many
manual workers, both skilled and unskilled, faced the prospect of
indefinite unemployment. For their wives there was the impossible
task of trying to feed families and keep homes warm on the money
provided by paltry social security benefits. However, such problems
were not to be limited to the working class: this Depression also
dragged down the middle classes. From the small-scale shopkeepers

to the graduate professionals in law and medicine, people struggled to survive in a world where their goods and services were decreasingly in demand. For such casualties the decline in their economic position was further accentuated by the loss of pride and respectability, which accompanied poverty and unemployment. In the countryside the situation was no better than in the towns. As world demand contracted further, the agricultural depression deepened markedly, leading to widespread rural poverty. For some tenant farmers there was even the ultimate ignominy of eviction from tenancies which had been in their families for generations.

In the relative prosperity of today it is difficult to appreciate the scale of the economic and social suffering which struck Germany in the early 1930s. To many ordinary respectable Germans it must have seemed as if society itself was breaking down uncontrollably and it is perhaps not so surprising that many people lost faith in the Weimar Republic, which seemed to offer no end to the misery, and began to see salvation in the solutions offered by political extremism. In this way the economic crisis in Germany quickly degenerated into a more obvious political crisis.

6 Nazi Electoral Breakthrough

> **KEY ISSUE** How and why did the Nazi Party emerge as a national political force in the years 1929–30?

In 1929 the German government was in the hands of Hermann Müller's Grand Coalition, which had been formed after the general election of May 1928. Yet, at the very time when unity and firm government were required to tackle the economic crisis, the Weimar Republic was being torn apart by the resurrection of the emotive issue of reparations.

The Dawes Plan (1924) successfully overcame the reparations crisis of the early 1920s by rescheduling payments based on Germany's capacity to pay, but from the outset it was seen as a temporary measure until Germany regained its economic strength. In early 1929 the IARC (Inter-Allied Reparations Commission) formed a committee of international financiers under the chairmanship of the American banker Owen Young. Its report in June 1929 suggested a new scheme of payments. Germany was to continue paying reparations until 1988, but the final sum was reduced to £1,850 million (only one-quarter of the figure demanded in 1921). After some negotiation, during which Stresemann had procured an Allied promise to evacuate the Rhineland by June 1930, the Young Plan was accepted by the government.

However, in right-wing circles, Stresemann's achievement was seen as yet another betrayal of German interests to the Allies. In their view any payment of reparations was based upon the 'lie' of Germany's war guilt (Article 231 of the Treaty of Versailles) and therefore the new scheme had to be opposed. A national committee, led by the new leader of the Nationalists, Alfred Hugenberg, was formed to fight the Young Plan. Hugenberg was also Germany's greatest media tycoon. He owned 150 newspapers and a publishing house, as well as the world-famous UFA film organisation. He now used all his resources to promote his message. Moreover, he generated support from a wide variety of right-wing factions – the *Stahlhelm* (the largest ex-servicemen's organisation), the Pan-German League, leading industrialists and Hitler's Nazis. Together this 'National Opposition' drafted a *Law against the Enslavement of the German People* which denounced any payment of reparations and demanded the punishment of any minister agreeing to such a treaty. The proposal gained enough signatures for it to be made the issue of a national referendum in December 1929. In the end the 'National Opposition' won only 5.8 million votes, a long way short of the 21 million required by the constitution for success. However, the campaign had stirred nationalist emotions, focusing opposition on the democratic government at a vital time. It had also brought together many right-wing opponents of the Republic and, perhaps most important of all for the future, it had given Hitler and the Nazis a national standing for the first time.

Müller's government successfully withstood the attack from the 'National Opposition'. However, it was not so resilient to its own internal divisions. Müller, a Social Democrat, struggled to hold the coalition together and not surprisingly, it was an issue of government finance which finally brought down the government in March 1930. The sharp increase in unemployment had created a large deficit in the insurance scheme, and the four parties in the coalition could not reconcile their differences on how to tackle it. The Social Democrats (SPD), as the political representatives of the trade unions, wanted to increase the contributions and to maintain the levels of welfare payments. The People's Party (DVP), on the other hand, had strong ties with big business and insisted on reducing benefits. Müller had no option but to tender the resignation of his government.

President Hindenburg appointed Heinrich Brüning as the new Chancellor. At first sight this appeared an obvious choice, since he was the parliamentary leader of the Centre Party, the second largest party in the Reichstag. However, with hindsight, it seems clear that Brüning's elevation marked the end of true parliamentary government, for he was manoeuvred into office by the select circle of political intriguers who now surrounded the ageing President; Otto Meissner, the President's State Secretary, Oskar von Hindenburg, the President's son, and Major General Kurt von Schleicher, the political voice of the Army, had all lost faith in the democratic process.

Instead, they looked to the President and the emergency powers of Article 48 of the constitution as a means of creating an authoritarian government backed by the Army. In Brüning they saw a respectable conservative figure, who also believed in the necessity of firm leadership. Initially he hoped to achieve this by heading a centre-right coalition, which excluded the Social Democrats.

Brüning's response to the growing economic crisis was to propose cuts in government expenditure, so as to achieve a balanced budget and to avoid any risk of rekindling inflation. It was rejected in the Reichstag by 256 votes to 193 in July 1930. In this situation Brüning put the proposals into effect by means of an emergency decree signed by the President according to Article 48. The Reichstag challenged the legality of this action and voted for the withdrawal of the decree. Deadlock had been reached. Brüning therefore asked Hindenburg to dissolve the Reichstag and to call an election for September 1930.

	1928	1930	1932 (July)	1932 (Nov)
Total on register (in millions)	41.2	43.0	44.2	44.4
Size of poll (per cent)	75.6	82.0	84.1	80.6
Total number of Reichstag seats	491	577	608	584
Nazis (NSDAP)	12	107	230	196
Nationalists (DNVP)	73	41	37	52
People's Party (DVP)	45	30	7	11
Centre Party (ZP)	78	87	97	90
Democratic Party (DDP)	25	20	4	2
Social Democrats (SPD)	153	143	133	121
Communists KPD	54	77	89	100
Others	51	72	11	12

Table of Weimar Election Results

He was hopeful that in the developing crisis the electorate would be encouraged to back his centre-right coalition. The election results proved him wrong. The real beneficiary was the Nazi Party, which increased its vote from 810,000 to a staggering 6,409,600.

After the disappointing overall result of the 1928 Reichstag election, no-one – not even Hitler – had expected the dramatic gains of September 1930. However, since 1928 the Nazi leaders had deliberately directed their propaganda at rural and middle-class/lower middle-class audiences and with 107 seats in 1930 the Nazis had become the second largest political party in Germany. This was achieved partly at the expense of the Nationalists (DNVP), whose vote was halved, and partly by the decline of the middle-class democratic parties, the Democrats (DDP) and the People's Party (DVP), who lost 20 seats between them. But Nazi success cannot just be explained by these 'protest votes'. It has been estimated that nearly half of the Nazi seats were won by the Party attracting new voters. The electorate had grown by 1.8 million since the previous election, and the turn-out had increased from 76.5 per cent to 82 per cent. It would seem that the Nazis had not only picked up a fair proportion of these young first-time voters, but had also persuaded many people who had not previously participated in elections to support their cause.

7 The Advent of Presidential Government

> **KEY ISSUE** Why did it prove so difficult to achieve any degree of political stability in Germany in the years 1930–32?

a) Brüning

Brüning's political position after the election was undoubtedly very difficult. His plan of reinforcing his parliamentary support from the centre-right had not succeeded. Instead, he faced the uncompromising opposition of the more powerful extremes of left and right. However, he was not unseated as Chancellor. He still enjoyed the support of Hindenburg and the Social Democrats decided to 'tolerate' his use of Article 48 (though not to join his government) because of the threat now facing the republic from the extremists. In this way true parliamentary democracy gave way to presidential government with a degree of backing from the Reichstag.

It seems that Brüning's aims were firstly, to end the payment of reparations and to accelerate the revision of the Versailles treaty and secondly, to strengthen the executive at the expense of the Reichstag. In the long run he almost certainly wanted to create a more authoritarian regime. By pursuing the strong deflationary programme, he hoped to demonstrate to the Allies that the payment of reparations was no longer possible. In this he succeeded, for reparations were eventually abolished by the Lausanne Conference of June 1932 – ironically a few days after Brüning's resignation. Similarly, he pursued the idea of the Austro-German Customs Union, partly as a sop to nationalist desires for the *Anschluss* (the union of Germany and Austria), but also to encourage a revival in trade. But the announcement of such a scheme in March 1931 backfired badly. France referred the proposal to the International Court of Justice on the grounds that it was contrary to the terms of the Treaty of Versailles, and the judges supported France's objection by eight votes to seven. This was a major blow for Brüning and his Foreign Minister, Curtius, felt compelled to resign.

However, Brüning was not astute enough to recognise how dangerous and unstable the politico-economic crisis had become in Germany. In June 1931 one of Germany's major banks, the Danat, closed its doors to customers. By early 1932 unemployment had topped 5 million. Increasingly, political tensions were played out in the streets where the private political armies clashed. Moreover, he did not face up to the precarious nature of his own position which depended solely on retaining the confidence of the President.

Brüning's last act was to secure the re-election of President Hindenburg whose first seven-year term of office came to an end in the spring of 1932. The Nazis fought a very effective campaign, but it was Hindenburg who won. He polled 19.3 million votes (53 per cent), Hitler 13.4 million (36.8 per cent) and Thälmann, the Communist, 3.7 million (10.2 per cent). However, it was a negative victory. Hindenburg had only been elected because the alternatives were too frightening. Moreover, there was no certainty that he had either the ability or the desire to stand by the democratic constitution. On the other hand, Hitler, despite losing, had doubled the Nazi vote and had projected a powerful personal image.

Hindenburg showed no gratitude to Brüning for supporting his re-election. At the end of May 1932 the President forced his Chancellor's resignation by refusing to sign any more emergency decrees. It is generally agreed that this decision had been prompted by the group surrounding the old man. Schleicher, recognising Brüning's failures, had become convinced that the Nazis could no longer be ignored and must be included as part of a more right-wing government which did not rely on the 'toleration' of the Social Democrats. The President finally succumbed to this line of argument when news broke of Brüning's latest economic proposal to deploy 600,000 unemployed workers on *Junker* estates in East Prussia. Such a plan was portrayed as 'agrarian bolshevism' in landowning circles, and it provided the perfect opportunity for Schleicher to engineer Brüning's fall.

Brüning was an honest, hard-working and honourable man who failed. He was not really a committed democrat, but neither was he sympathetic to Nazism. The extent to which his failure should be seen as his responsibility, and how much as the result of circumstances and forces beyond his control, remains a matter of some conjecture. But there is little doubt that the overall effect of his two years in charge of the government was to accustom the public to rule by decree and thereby to significantly undermine democracy.

b) Papen

The new Chancellor, Franz von Papen, had been suggested to Hindenburg by Schleicher. As an aristocrat Papen had good connections with high society; as a Catholic he was a member of the Centre Party, although his political views mirrored those of the Nationalists. Such 'virtues' quickly formed the basis for a close friendship between Hindenburg and Papen. Papen was also politically ambitious, but his understanding and experience of politics was limited (he did not even hold a seat in the Reichstag!). If the choice of Papen was greeted with incredulity by many, it was the man's very lack of expertise which appealed to Schleicher, who saw the opportunity to influence events more directly through him. The new cabinet, soon nicknamed the 'Cabinet of Barons', was dominated by aristocratic landowners and industrialists. However, Schleicher had also extracted a promise from Hitler that the Nazis would not oppose the new government in return for two concessions: the dissolution of the Reichstag and the calling of fresh elections; and the ending of a government ban on the SA and SS, which had been introduced in the wake of violence during the presidential campaign. In this way Schleicher hoped to achieve his objective of a right-wing authoritarian government with a measure of popular support in the form of the Nazis. The Reichstag was therefore dissolved, and an election was arranged to take place on 31 July 1932.

The campaign which followed the announcement of the election was brutal, as street violence once again took hold in the large cities. In the month of July alone 86 people died as a result of political fights. Such bloodshed provided Schleicher and Papen with the excuse to abolish the state government of Prussia on 20 July on the grounds of its ineffectiveness. The coalition of Centre and Social Democrats there had been a focus of right-wing resentment since 1919, but it was now removed by Papen simply declaring a state of emergency and appointing himself Reich Commissioner of Prussia. This was an arbitrary and unconstitutional act, and yet the Social Democrats (and the trade unions) gave in without opposition. Whether resistance would have achieved anything is debatable, but their passive response is indicative of the extent to which the forces of democracy had lost the initiative.

Many on the right wing congratulated Papen on the Prussian *coup*. However, it does not seem to have won him any additional electoral support. When the election results came in, it was again the Nazis who had cause to celebrate. They had polled 13.7 million votes and had won 230 seats. Hitler was the leader of by far the largest party in Germany and constitutionally he had every right to form a government.

8 Nazi Voters

KEY ISSUE Who voted for the Nazis and why?

The point is often made that Hitler and the Nazis never gained an overall majority in Reichstag elections. However, such an occurrence was unlikely because of the number of political parties in Weimar Germany and the operation of the proportional representation system. Considering this, Nazi electoral achievements by July 1932 were quite staggering. The 13,745,000 voters who had supported them represented 37.4 per cent of the electorate, thus making Hitler's party the largest in the Reichstag. Only one other party on one other occasion had polled more – the SPD in the revolutionary atmosphere of January 1919. Nazism had become a mass movement with which millions identified, and as such it laid the foundations for Hitler's coming to power in January 1933. Who were these Nazi voters and why were they attracted to the Nazi cause?

It has already been suggested that the Nazis won more support from new voters and previous non-voters than from other parties, and this trend was to continue until March 1933. However, such an explanation is insufficient on its own. If you study the table on page 25 a number of points emerge.

It seems fairly clear that the Nazis made extensive gains from those parties with a middle-class and/or a Protestant identity. However, it is also apparent that the Catholic parties, the Communist Party and, to a large extent, the Social Democrats were able to withstand the Nazi advances. These trends are further reflected in the geographical base of Nazi support which was generally higher in the north and east of the country and lower in the south and west. Right across the North German Plain, from East Prussia to Schleswig-Holstein, the Nazis gained their best results and this seems to reflect the significance of two important factors – religion and the degree of urbanisation. In those areas where Catholicism predominated, the Nazi breakthrough was less marked, whereas the more Protestant regions were more likely to vote Nazi. Likewise, the Nazis fared less well in the large industrial cities, but gained greater support in the more rural communities and in residential suburbs. Consequently, the Nazi vote was at its lowest in the Catholic cities of the west, such as Cologne and Düsseldorf. It was at its highest in the Protestant countryside of the north and north-east, such as Schleswig-Holstein and Pomerania.

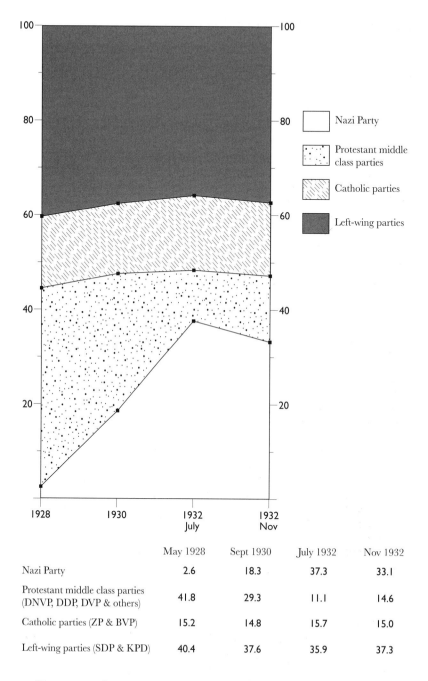

	May 1928	Sept 1930	July 1932	Nov 1932
Nazi Party	2.6	18.3	37.3	33.1
Protestant middle class parties (DNVP, DDP, DVP & others)	41.8	29.3	11.1	14.6
Catholic parties (ZP & BVP)	15.2	14.8	15.7	15.0
Left-wing parties (SDP & KPD)	40.4	37.6	35.9	37.3

Percentage of vote gained by each major political grouping, 1928–32.

Ironically, therefore, Bavaria, a strongly Catholic region, and the birth-place of Nazism, had one of the lowest Nazi votes in Germany. Such a picture does not of course take into account the exceptions created by local circumstances. For instance, parts of the province of Silesia, though mainly Catholic and urbanised, still recorded a very high Nazi vote (probably the result of nationalist passions generated in a border province which had lost half its land to Poland).

Why were those with an allegiance to Catholicism or socialism not so readily drawn in to voting for the Nazis? Firstly, both of them represented well-established ideologies in their own right and both opposed Nazism on an intellectual level. Secondly, the organisational strength of each movement provided an effective counter to Nazi propaganda: for socialism there was the trade union structure; for Catholicism there was the Church hierarchy, extending right down to the local parish priest. Thirdly, both movements had been attacked during the *Kaiserreich* and, as so often happens, persecution had resulted in a strengthening of group identity. It was therefore much harder for the Nazis to break down the traditional loyalties of working-class and Catholic communities. Their traditional 'associationism' was much stronger whereas the Protestants, the farmers and the middle classes were not so tied and were therefore perhaps more likely to accept the Nazi message.

However, such an analysis should not obscure the fact that the Nazis still boasted a broader cross-section of supporters than any other party. Unlike many other parties the Nazis were not constrained by regional, denominational and class ties so that by 1932 the NSDAP had become Germany's first genuine *Volkspartei* or broad-based people's party. The point was made in a recent study of voting habits that the Nazis only became a mass party by making some inroads into the working-class vote.[1] Hitler therefore succeeded in appealing to all sections of German society – it is simply that those from Protestant, rural and middle-class backgrounds sympathised in greater numbers.

What appears to have been common to many of the Nazi voters was a lack of faith in and identity with the existing system, and a belief that their traditional role and status in society was under threat. This kind of sociological interpretation also tends to substantiate the view that ideologically Nazism successfully portrayed itself as both revolutionary and reactionary, since it wished to destroy the republic while at the same time promising a return to a glorious bygone age. For the shopkeepers, craftsmen, farmers, white collar workers and many professional people, the crisis of 1929–33 was merely the climax of a series of disasters since 1918. Hitler was therefore able to exploit what is termed 'the politics of anxiety'. He seemed able to offer to many Germans an escape from overwhelming crisis and a return to respectability.

[By 1930] the NSDAP had become a unique phenomenon in German electoral politics, a catch-all party of protest, whose constituents, while drawn primarily from the middle class electorate were united above all by a profound contempt for the existing political and economic system.[2]

Another clearly identifiable group of Nazi sympathisers was the youth of Germany. The Depression hit at the moment when young-sters from the pre-war baby-boom came of age and however good their qualifications were, they had little chance of finding work. Although age does not stand out as a defining feature in voting analyses, it was a factor in Party membership: 41.3 per cent of those who became Party members before 1933 had been born between 1904 and 1913 – despite this age group representing only 25.3 per cent of the total population. Thus it was the young who filled the ranks of the SA – often unemployed, disillusioned and without hope for the future, many youngsters saw Nazism as a movement for change. And the SA activities gave them something to do! It would seem that all ages were prepared to vote for the Nazis, but the younger members of society were actually more likely to become involved by joining the Party.[3]

It is possible therefore to come to some tentative conclusions about who voted for the Nazis and perhaps why. However, statistics may be presented and interpreted in a variety of ways, while sociological explanations can easily degenerate into simplistic generalisations which fail to take into account the widely differing views that existed. Support for the Nazis was actually quite unstable. Membership lists seem to have frequently fluctuated and the Party's electoral support was actually highly volatile which probably reflects the severity of the crisis facing Germany.

9 Nazi Political Methods

KEY ISSUE How did the Nazis exploit the political circumstances to their advantage?

Even so, it would be naive to assume that voters for the Nazi Party were simply won over by the appeal of a radical political ideology at a time of economic crisis. There were numerous other fringe parties on the extreme right which publicised similar messages. What differenti-ated the Nazis and ensured that it was them the voters chose was their revolutionary political style or, to use present-day jargon, the presen-tation and packaging of the Party and its programme.

From his earliest days in politics Hitler had shown an uncanny but cynical awareness of the power of propaganda. In 1924 in *Mein Kampf* he had written:

I The receptive powers of the masses are very restricted, and their understanding is feeble. On the other hand, they quickly forget. Such

being the case, all effective propaganda must be confined to a few bare
essentials and those must be expressed as far as possible in stereotyped
5 formulas. These slogans should be persistently repeated until the very
last individual has come to grasp the idea that has been put forward.

Such thinking was to remain the basis of Nazi propaganda, and there
can be little doubt that its implementation in the years 1929–33
played a vital part in Nazi success.

The whole process of Nazi propaganda was highly organised. From
April 1930 Joseph Goebbels was put in charge of a propaganda
machine which reached right down to branch level. In this way information and instructions could be sent out from Party headquarters
and adapted to local circumstances. It also allowed the Party to target
its money and efforts on the key electoral districts. Finally, it encouraged feed-back from the grass-roots, so that particularly effective ideas
could be put into practice elsewhere.

Above all, it was the range of propaganda techniques and their
increasingly sophisticated application which marked a new approach
in electioneering. Posters and leaflets had always played an important
role, but now the electorate was deluged with them. The Nazis practised mass politics on a grand scale, whilst showing a subtlety and an
understanding of psychology which we now associate with advertising
agencies. The following directive was issued by the Reich Propaganda
Department to all *Gau* Propaganda Departments during the presidential campaign of 1932:

1 ... Hitler Poster. The Hitler poster depicts a fascinating Hitler head on
a completely black background. Subtitle: white on black – 'Hitler'. In
accordance with the Führer's wish this poster is to be put up only
during the final days (of the campaign). Since experience shows that
5 during the final days there is a variety of coloured posters, this poster
with its completely black background will contrast with all the others
and will produce a tremendous effect on the masses ...

Modern technology was also beginning to be exploited.
Loudspeakers, radio, film and records were all used. Expensive cars
and aeroplanes were hired, not only for the practical purpose of
transporting Hitler quickly to as many places as possible, but also to
project a statesman-like image. In 1932 three major speaking programmes were organised for Hitler called 'Flight over Germany'. At a
local level the political message was projected by the Party arranging
social events and entertainments – sports, concerts, fairs.

However, it was in the organisation of the mass rallies that the
Nazis showed their mastery of propaganda. The intention was to
create an atmosphere so emotional that all members of the crowd
would succumb to the collective will. This is the idea of 'mass suggestion' and every kind of device was used to heighten the effect: uniforms, torches, music, salutes, flags, songs and anthems, and speeches

Our Last Hope – Nazi Election poster.

from leading personalities. Many people have since described how they were converted as a result of such meetings.

The dominant themes of Nazi propaganda were firstly, the Führer cult in which Hitler was portrayed as a messiah-type figure and secondly, the unifying idea of a *Volksgemeinschaft*. Yet they also correctly recognised the need to direct propaganda according to people's social and economic interests. Specific leaflets were produced for different social groups, and Nazi speakers paid particular attention to the worries and concerns of the individual clubs and societies they addressed. In this way the Nazi propaganda message was tailored to fit a whole range of people; farmers, workers, the unemployed, shopkeepers and businessmen all came to see National Socialism in a slightly different way.

There was one other strand to this Nazi revolution in political style: the systematic encouragement and use of violence. Weimar politics had been a bloody affair from the start, but the growth of the SA and SS unleashed an unprecedented wave of violence, persecution and intimidation. During the campaign of July 1932, there were 461 political riots in Prussia alone; battles between Communists and Nazis on 10 July left ten dead; a week later 19 died after the Nazis marched through a working-class suburb of Hamburg. Such activities were encouraged by the Nazi leadership, as control of the streets was seen as vital to the expansion of Nazi power. The ballot box of democracy remained merely a means to an end, and therefore other non-democratic tactics were considered legitimate in the quest for power. The Nazis poured scorn on rational discussion and fair play. For them the end did justify the means. For their democratic opponents, there was the dilemma of how to resist those who exploited the freedoms of a democratic society merely to undermine it.

10 The Appointment of Hitler as Chancellor

> **KEY ISSUE** Why did President Hindenburg eventually appoint Hitler as Chancellor?

The political strength of the Nazi Party following the July elections was beyond doubt. However, there still remained the problem for Hitler of how to translate this popular following into real power. He was determined to take nothing less than the post of Chancellor for himself. This was unacceptable to both Schleicher and Papen, who were keen to have Nazis in the cabinet but only in positions of limited power. Therefore, the meeting between Hitler, Papen and Hindenburg on 13 August ended in deadlock. While Papen retained the sympathy of Hindenburg, Hitler's ambitions would remain frustrated.

Noakes describes the period from August to December 1932 as 'the months of crisis' for the Nazis, since 'it appeared the policy of legality had led to a cul-de-sac'.[4] Party morale declined and some of the wilder SA elements became increasingly restless. Papen, on the other hand, grew confident that the political stalemate was undermining the position of the Nazis, who, he believed, had reached the zenith of their electoral support (an opinion shared by the British ambassador). Consequently, he dissolved the new Reichstag when it met on 12 September. In many respects Papen's reading of the situation was sound. The Nazis were short of money, their morale was low and the electorate was growing tired of all the elections. These factors undoubtedly contributed to the fall in the Nazi vote on 6 November to 11.7 million (33.1 per cent), which gave them 196 seats. However, Papen's tactics had not achieved their desired end, since the fundamental problem of overcoming the lack of majority Reichstag support for his cabinet remained. Hitler stood firm – he would not join the government except as Chancellor.

In his frustration, Papen began to consider a drastic alternative; the dissolution of the Reichstag, the declaration of martial law and the establishment of a presidential dictatorship. However, such a plan was anathema to Schleicher who found Papen's growing self-confidence, as well as his friendship with President Hindenburg, additional causes for concern. Schleicher still believed that the popular support for the Nazis could not be ignored, and that Papen's plan would give rise to civil commotion. When he informed Hindenburg of the Army's lack of confidence in Papen, the President was forced unwillingly to demand the resignation of his friendly Chancellor.

Schleicher at last came out into the open, and on 2 December Hindenburg appointed him Chancellor. His aim, rather ambitiously, was to create a more broadly based government by splitting the Nazis and attracting the more socialist wing of the Nazi Party, under Gregor Strasser, to support him. He hoped to gain some support from the left by a programme of public works. In this way Schleicher intended to project himself as the Chancellor of national reconciliation. However, his political manoeuvres came to nothing. The trade unions remained deeply suspicious of his motives and, encouraged by their political masters from the Social Democratic Party, broke off the negotiations. Strasser did respond to Schleicher's overtures, but Hitler retained the loyalty of the Party's leadership. This left Strasser isolated and he was forced to resign. Nevertheless, the incident had been a major blow to Party morale and tensions remained high in the last few weeks of 1932 as the prospect of achieving power seemed to drift away.

Hitler's fortunes did not begin to take a more favourable turn until the first week of 1933. Papen (and Hindenburg) had never forgiven Schleicher for the way he had been dropped. Papen was determined to regain political office and he now recognised that this could be achieved only by convincing President Hindenburg that he could muster majority support in the Reichstag. Consequently, secret contacts were made with Nazi leaders which culminated in a meeting on 4 January 1933 between Papen and Hitler. Here it was agreed in essence that Hitler should head a Nazi–Nationalist coalition government with Papen as Vice-Chancellor.

Back-stage intrigue to unseat Schleicher now took over. Papen looked for support for his plan from major landowners, leaders of industry and the Army. It was only now that the conservative establishment thought that they had identified an escape from the threat of communism and the dangerous intrigues of Schleicher. Above all though, Papen had to convince the President himself. Undoubtedly encouraged by his son Oskar and his State Secretary Meissner, Hindenburg eventually gave in. Schleicher had failed in his attempt to bring stability. In fact, he had only succeeded in frightening the powerful vested interests with his ambitious plans. Hindenburg, therefore, heeded the advice of Papen to make Hitler Chancellor of a coalition government, secure in the knowledge that the Nazis would be overwhelmed by traditional conservatives and Nationalists. On 28 January 1933 Hindenburg withdrew his support for Schleicher as Chancellor; two days later he appointed Hitler to head a coalition government of 'national concentration'.

11 Assessment

> **KEY ISSUE** Why did the Nazis replace the Weimar Republic?

In 1932 only 43 per cent of the electorate voted in the July Reichstag elections for pro-republican parties. The majority of the German people had voted in a free (and reasonably fair) election to reject democracy, despite the fact that there was no clear alternative. By this time Weimar's problems had accumulated to immense proportions: its creation out of military defeat; its association with the Treaty of Versailles; the compromise constitution; the on-going economic problems; and the political uncertainties created by short-lived coalition governments. However, its problems did not have to end in a Nazi dictatorship, so why was it that Hitler assumed the mantle of power just six months later?

The Depression had transformed the Nazis into a *mass* movement. Admittedly, 63 per cent of Germans never voted for them, but 37 per cent did, so that the Nazi Party became by far the strongest party in a multi-party democracy. The Depression had led to such profound social and economic hardship that it created an environment of discontent which, in conjunction with Weimar's other failings, could easily be exploited by the Nazis' style of political activity. Indeed, it must be questionable whether Hitler would have become a national political figure without the severity of the economic down-turn (that, of course, is not to say that the Weimar Republic would have survived in the long term). However, his mixture of racist, nationalist and anti-democratic ideas were readily received by a broad spectrum of German people, and especially by the disgruntled middle classes. There can be little doubt that Nazi ideology did successfully identify itself with certain populist fears and desires which had already found expression in the intellectual and cultural history of Germany over the previous century.

Yet, other extreme right-wing groups with similar ideas and conditions did not enjoy similar success. This is partially explained by the effective manner in which the Nazi message was communicated: the use of modern propaganda techniques; the violent exploitation of scapegoats, especially the Jews and communists; and the well-organised structure of the Party apparatus. All these factors undoubtedly helped, but in terms of electoral appeal it is impossible to ignore the powerful impact of Hitler himself as a charismatic leader with a cult following of almost messianic proportions. Furthermore, he exhibited a quite extraordinary political acumen and ruthlessness when he was involved in the minutiae of political in-fighting.

Nevertheless, the huge popular following of the Nazis, which so vitally undermined the continued operation of democracy, was insufficient on its own to give Hitler power. In the final analysis, it was the mutual recognition by Hitler and the representatives of the traditional leaders of the Army, the landowners and heavy industry that they needed each other which led to Hitler's appointment as Chancellor of a coalition government on 30 January 1933. Ever since September 1930 every government had been forced to resort almost continuously to the use of presidential emergency decrees because they lacked a popular mandate. In the chaos of 1932 the only other realistic alternative to including the Nazis in the government was some kind of military regime – a presidential dictatorship backed by the Army, perhaps. However, that too would have faced similar difficulties – indeed, by failing to satisfy the extreme left and the extreme right there would have been a very real possibility of civil war. A coalition with Hitler's Nazis therefore provided the conservative elites with both mass support and some alluring promises: a vigorous attack on Germany's political left wing; and rearmament as a precursor to economic and political expansion abroad. For Hitler, the inclusion of Papen, Hugenberg and von Blomberg gave his cabinet an air of conservative respectability. In the end, Hitler became Chancellor because the political forces of the left and centre were respectively too divided and too weak, and because the conservative right wing was prepared to accept him as a partner in government in the mistaken belief that he could be tamed. With hindsight, it can be seen that 30 January 1933 was decisive. The dictatorship did not start technically until the completion of the 'legal revolution' in February–March 1933, but Hitler was already entrenched in power and, as one historian has claimed, now he 'could only be removed by an earthquake'.[5]

References

1   J. Falter, *Hitlers Wähler* (Munich, 1991) pp. 287–9
2   T. Childers, *The Nazi Voter. The Social foundations of Fascism in Germany* (London, 1983) p. 268
3   See Falter, op. cit.
4   Noakes & Pridham, *Nazism 1919–45*, Vol. 1 (Exeter, 1983) p. 105
5   F. Carsten, *The Rise of Fascism* (Cambridge, 1967) p. 153

Summary Diagram
Hitler and the Nazi Party – the road to power

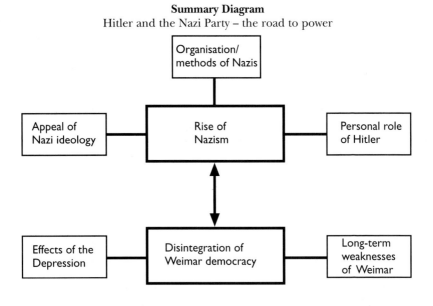

There is a lot of ground to be covered in this chapter in terms of both content and analysis. A good understanding is essential, for not only is the material very likely to form the basis for an exam question in its own right, but it is also a valuable complement to those who have studied Weimar history. The level of detail required from your notes in this chapter therefore needs to be thought about carefully. Your major objective is to understand the complex causation underlying one of the great historical debates. But there is no denying that unless you also appreciate the events and personalities of 1929 you will remain rather confused.

First of all, to gain a good overview, copy out the summary diagram, whilst leaving plenty of space all around it. By referring back to the text, see if you can add four or five relevant examples/details to each of the smaller boxes. Now try to deepen your understanding further by carrying out the following tasks:

i) Construct a brief timeline of Hitler's life and career up to 1924. Then in about 150 words write a character sketch of the man focusing on what you consider to have been the major influences on him.

ii) Take each of the events mentioned under the Key Dates on page 9 and describe each one in some detail. But also explain the significance/importance of each event and how it contributed to the rise of Nazism.

iii) Study the tables on pages 20 and 25. Write an 'election analysis' (you could do this by explaining the fortunes of one party at a time or by considering each election in turn).

iv) Examine individually the roles of Hindenburg, Brüning, Papen and Schleicher. Explain why each one was unable to provide effective leadership in the crisis.

v) Re-read section 11 very carefully and, without reference to the text, write a summary in no more than 150 words.

Answering structured and essay questions on Chapter 2

Many of the questions you will be expected to answer on the topic covered in this chapter will be variations and combinations of 'How and why did Hitler and the Nazis rise to power?' If you are answering a structured question it will tend to pinpoint a particular aspect of the topic. Look at the following questions:

1. a) Outline the main events of the Beer Hall *putsch* in 1923.
     b) Explain why its failure did not mark the end of Hitler's political career.
2. a) Outline the main elements of Nazi ideology.
     b) Why did the Nazis enjoy only limited political success in the years 1924–9?
3. a) Outline the main features of the economic crisis which hit Germany during 1930–2.
     b) Who supported Hitler and the Nazis and why?

You will see that in each case the first part asks you to display your historical knowledge of the topic. As long as you write accurately and relevantly you should score good marks. The second part requires you to think more because you need to select the facts and information and apply them to answering a more analytical question.

Essay questions are likely to be more broadly based and they will be framed more specifically around the key issue of why. For example:

1. Why was Hitler able to come to power only ten years after the failed Munich *putsch* of 1923?

2. How do you explain the appeal of the Nazi Party to German voters between 1930 and 1932?
3. Why did Hindenburg finally appoint Hitler Chancellor in January 1933?
4. Why did Hitler become the most powerful opponent of the Weimar Republic?

You must not be tempted to write a descriptive narrative. Instead, you must use the wealth of factual material as evidence for your analysis. A good way to tackle such explanatory questions is to draw up a list based upon a number of reasons or factors which start with the word 'because'. For example, in question 4, you could include the following:

because of the effects of the Depression
because of his personal charisma
because of the Party's organisation/structure
because of Nazi propaganda

What other reasons or factors would you include?
When you have compiled a list, try to arrange the items into logical sets such as: long-term, short-term and immediate causes; or political, economic, and social factors. This will provide you with an essay plan divided into three or four organised sections – one for each set. Draw up such a plan for question 4. In writing your essay, develop each of the sections, including the historical details, to support your argument. However, it is very important to realise that you will have to be selective in your choice of factual material. In a typical examination essay of 45 minutes you will probably have no more than ten minutes per section! You must therefore exploit only the most relevant historical detail, bearing in mind the demands of the question and the limits of time. It is no good writing a brilliant first section if you only have fifteen minutes left for the other three! Good essay planning should help you to overcome the problems of timing in the examination room.

Finally, the essay will require a conclusion. It is all too easy with an explanatory essay to use the final paragraph merely to summarise your points. This is unlikely to earn you any extra marks because you are not adding anything of importance to your answer. So, in your conclusion try to assess what you consider to be the most significant cause(s). Alternatively, show how the various factors relate to each other. This is important because a well-ordered explanatory essay can too easily appear as a series of water-tight compartments. Historical causation is normally about the inter-action of forces, and it would be a good idea for your conclusion to try to reflect this.

Source-based questions on Chapter 2

1. The Nazi Party 25-point Programme of 1920
Carefully read the extracts from the programme on page 11. Answer the following questions:

a) Explain in your own words what the Nazis meant by the word *Volk*. (*2 marks*)
b) Which of the points do you consider to be i) nationalist ii) racist and iii) socialist? Explain your answer in each case. (*8 marks*)
c) In what ways does the Party programme attempt to appeal to the fears and prejudices of the German people? (*5 marks*)
d) What are the strengths and weaknesses of the extract as evidence of Nazi political intentions? (*5 marks*)

2. *Hitler's* **Mein Kampf**

Carefully read the extracts from *Mein Kampf* on pages 13 and 14–15. Answer the following questions:

a) Explain what Hitler meant by i) 'the force which France now deprives us of' (page 15 lines 21–22), and ii) 'the plough is then the sword' (page 14 line 8). (*4 marks*)
b) From these two extracts what do you consider to have been Hitler's strongest political emotion? Explain your answer. (*5 marks*)
c) On the basis of these two extracts, what do you consider to have been the strengths and weaknesses of *Mein Kampf* as a piece of political propaganda? (*4 marks*)
d) Hitler's policies on race and foreign affairs remained remarkably constant from 1924 to 1933. How do you explain the fact that National Socialism only achieved national prominence after 1930? (*7 marks*)

3. *Nazi Use of Propaganda*

Read the extracts from *Mein Kampf* and the Propaganda Department on pages 27 and 28. Study the election poster on page 29. Answer the following questions:

a) Explain in your own words how Hitler viewed the electorate. (*4 marks*)
b) At whom is the poster directed? In what ways does the poster try to gain the support of the electorate? (*5 marks*)
c) How far does the poster reflect the attitudes expressed in the two written extracts? (*4 marks*)
d) The Nazis placed enormous importance on the role of propaganda. How significant really was propaganda in the political success of National Socialism? (*7 marks*)

3 The Nazi Consolidation of Power, 1933–4

POINTS TO CONSIDER

Your main aim when reading this chapter for the first time should be to understand how, by the summer of 1934, Germany became a one-party state under the dictatorial leadership of Hitler. As you do this, it is important for you to a) recognise the range of competing political forces and b) appreciate the significance of each of the key turning-points in the Nazi consolidation of power.

KEY DATES

1933	30 Jan	Hitler appointed Chancellor.
	27 Feb	Reichstag fire: Communists blamed.
	5 Mar	Last elections according to Weimar constitution.
	21 Mar	Day of Potsdam.
	23 Mar	Enabling Act passed.
	14 July	All political opposition to NSDAP declared illegal.
1934	30 June	Night of the Long Knives: destruction of SA by SS.
	2 Aug	Death of Hindenburg: Hitler combined the offices of Chancellor and President. Oath of loyalty taken by Army.

1 The 'Legal Revolution'

> **KEY ISSUE** What does Bracher mean when he describes the events of January–March 1933 as 'a legal revolution'?

Although Hitler had been appointed Chancellor, his power was by no means absolute. Hindenburg had not been prepared to sanction Hitler's appointment until he had been satisfied that the Chancellor's power would remain limited. Such was Papen's confidence about Hitler's restricted room for manoeuvre that he boasted to a friend, 'In two months we'll have pushed Hitler into a corner so hard that he'll be squeaking'.[1]

At first sight the confidence of the conservatives seemed to be justified, since Hitler's position in purely constitutional terms was not strong. Firstly, there were only two other Nazis in the cabinet of 12 – Wilhelm Frick as Minister of the Interior, and Hermann Göring as a minister without portfolio. Secondly, Hitler's coalition government did not have a majority in the Reichstag. Thirdly, the Chancellor's post, as the previous 12 months had clearly shown, was dependent on the whim of President Hindenburg, and he openly resented Hitler. Yet, within two months these limitations were shown to be ineffectual, and Hitler had effectively become a dictator. Moreover, this was to be achieved by a continuation of the policy of legality which the Party had pursued since 1925. How and why did this happen?

Hitler already possessed several key advantages when he became Chancellor. He was the leader of the largest political party in Germany, and it had already been shown that a policy of ignoring him did not work. During 1932 it had only led to the ineffectual governments of Papen and Schleicher. Therefore, political realism forced the conservatives to work with him. They probably needed him more than he needed them. The alternative to Hitler was civil war or a Communist *coup* – or so it seemed to many people at the time. More importantly perhaps, the Nazi Party had now gained access to the resources of the state. For example, Göring not only had a place in the cabinet but was also Minister of the Interior in Prussia, with responsibility for the police. It was a responsibility which he used blatantly to harass opponents, while ignoring Nazi excesses. Goebbels, likewise, exploited the propaganda opportunities on behalf of the Nazis. 'The struggle is a light one now,' he confided in his diary, 'since we are able to employ all the means of the State. Radio and Press are at our disposal.' Above all, however, Hitler was a masterly political tactician, and he was determined to achieve absolute power for himself. It soon became clear that Papen's political puppet was too clever to be strung along by a motley collection of ageing conservatives.

a) The Reichstag Election of 5 March 1933

Hitler lost no time in removing his strings. Within 24 hours of his appointment as Chancellor, new Reichstag elections had been called. A somewhat half-hearted attempt had been made to gain the backing of the Centre Party, but Hitler did not want any more conditions placed upon him. Anyway, he felt new elections would not only increase the Nazi vote but would also enhance his own status.

The campaign for the last Reichstag elections held according to the Weimar constitution had few of the characteristics expected of liberal democracy: violence and terror dominated; and meetings of the Socialists and Communists were regularly broken up. In Prussia, Göring used his authority to enrol an extra 50,000 into the police – nearly all were members of the SA and SS! Altogether 69 people died during the five-week campaign. However, the atmosphere of hate and fear generated by the Nazis was also used to great effect in their election propaganda. Hitler set the tone in his 'Appeal to the German People' of 31 January 1933. He blamed the prevailing conditions on democratic government and the terrorist activities of the Communists. He cultivated the idea of the government as a 'National Uprising' determined to restore Germany's pride and unity. In this

Hitler's 'Appeal to the German People', 31 January 1933

1 Over 14 years have passed since that unhappy day when the German people, blinded by promises made by those at home and abroad, forgot the highest values of our past, of the Reich, of its honour and its freedom, and thereby lost everything. Since those days of treason, the
5 Almighty has withdrawn his blessing from our nation. Discord and hatred have moved in. Filled with the deepest distress, millions of the best German men and women from all walks of life see the unity of the nation disintegrating in a welter of egoistical political opinions, economic interests and ideological conflicts ...
10 The misery of our people is terrible! The starving industrial proletariat have become unemployed in their millions, while the whole middle and artisan class have been made paupers. If the German farmer also is involved in this collapse we shall be faced with a catastrophe of vast proportions. For in that case, there will collapse not only a Reich, but also
15 a 2,000-year-old inheritance of the highest works of human culture and civilisation ...
It is an appalling inheritance which we are taking over. The task before us is the most difficult which has faced German statesmen in living memory. But we all have unbounded confidence, for we believe in our
20 nation and in its eternal values. Farmers, workers and the middle class must unite to contribute the bricks wherewith to build the new Reich.
The National Government will therefore regard it as its first and supreme task to restore to the German people unity of mind and will. It will preserve and defend the foundations on which the strengths of
25 our nation rest. It will take under its firm protection Christianity as the basis of our morality, and the family as the nucleus of our nation and state. Standing above estates and classes, it will bring back to our people the consciousness of its racial and political unity and the obligations arising therefrom ... It will therefore declare merciless war on
30 spiritual, political and cultural nihilism. Germany must not and will not sink into Communist anarchy.
In fourteen years the November parties have ruined the German farmer. In fourteen years they created an army of millions of unemployed. The National Government will carry out the following plan with
35 iron resolution and dogged perseverance. Within four years the German farmer must be saved from pauperism. Within four years unemployment must be overcome. Parallel with this, there emerge the prerequisites for the recovery of the economy ... The Government of the National Uprising wishes to set to work, and it will work. It has not for fourteen
40 years brought ruin to the German nation; it wants to lead it to the summit. It is determined to make amends in four years for the liabilities of fourteen years.
But it cannot subject the work of reconstruction to the will of those who were responsible for the breakdown. The Marxist parties and their
45 followers had fourteen years to prove their abilities. The result is a heap of ruins. Now, German people, give us four years and then judge us. Let us begin, loyal to the command of the Field Marshal. May Almighty God favour our work, shape our will in the right way, bless our vision and bless us with the trust of our people. We have no desire to fight for ourselves;
50 only for Germany.

way he played on the inner-most desires of many Germans, but never committed himself to the details of a political and economic programme.

Another key difference in this election campaign was the improved Nazi financial situation. Many contemporary commentators on the left wing had long portrayed Hitler as a pawn of big business, which was said to be pouring money into the Party's coffers. However, recent research by Turner suggests that it was only after Hitler became Chancellor that the big donations from commerce and industry came flooding in.[2] At a meeting on 20 February with 20 leading industrialists, Hitler was promised three million Reichsmarks and with such financial backing and Goebbels' exploitation of the media, the Nazis were confident of securing a parliamentary majority.

As the campaign moved towards its climax, one further bizarre episode strengthened the Nazi hand. On 27 February the Reichstag building was set on fire, and a young Dutch Communist, van der Lubbe, was arrested in incriminating circumstances. At the time it was believed by many that the incident was a Nazi plot to substantiate the claims of an impending Communist *coup*, and thereby to justify Nazi repression. However, to this day the episode has defied satisfactory explanation. A major investigation in 1962 concluded that van der Lubbe had acted alone; but eighteen years later the West Berlin authorities posthumously acquitted him. It is probable that the true explanation will never be known, although there can be little doubt about the cynical way in which the Nazis exploited the incident to their advantage.

On the next day, 28 February, Frick drew up and Hindenburg signed the 'Decree for the Protection of People and State'. In a few short clauses most civil and political liberties were suspended and the power of central government strengthened – ostensibly because of the threat posed by the Communists. Following this, in the last week of the election campaign, hundreds of the Nazis' political opponents were arrested, and the violence reached new heights.

In this atmosphere of intimidation Germany went to the polls on 5 March. Somewhat surprisingly, the Nazis only increased their vote from 33.1 per cent to 43.9 per cent, thereby securing 288 seats. Hitler could only claim a majority in the new Reichstag with the help of the 52 seats won by the Nationalists. It was not only disappointing, it was also a political blow since any change in the existing Weimar Constitution required a two-thirds majority in the Reichstag.

b) The Enabling Act, March 1933

Despite this constitutional hurdle, Hitler decided to propose to the new Reichstag an Enabling Bill which would effectively do away with parliamentary procedure and legislation and which would instead transfer full powers to the Chancellor and his government for four years. In this way the dictatorship would be grounded in legality. However, the successful passage of the Enabling Bill was wholly dependent upon the support or abstention of other political parties.

A further problem was created by the fact that the momentum built up within the lower ranks of the Party during the election campaign was proving difficult for Hitler to contain. This was the so-called 'revolution from below'. It threatened to destroy Hitler's image of legality, and antagonise the conservative vested interests and his Nationalist allies. Such was his concern that a grandiose act of reassurance was arranged. On 21 March at Potsdam Garrison Church, Goebbels orchestrated the ceremony to celebrate the opening of the Reichstag. In the presence of Hindenburg, the Crown Prince (the son of Kaiser Wilhelm II), and many of the Army's leading generals, Hitler aligned National Socialism with the forces of the old Germany. The 'Day of Potsdam' was later described by Erich Ebermeyer:

1   How marvellously it's been staged by that master producer Goebbels. The procession of Hindenburg, the Government, and the deputies goes from Berlin to Potsdam past a solid line of cheering millions. The whole of Berlin seems to be on the streets ... The radio announcer almost
5   weeps with emotion.

    Then Hindenburg reads his speech. Plain, strong, coming from a simple heart and so presumably speaking to simple hearts ... he now, soon to die, presides over the marriage of his world with the new rising one which the Austrian corporal, Hitler, represents. Then Hitler
10   speaks. It cannot be denied. He has grown in stature. Out of the demagogue and party leader, the fanatic and agitator ... a true statesman seems to be developing ... The Government's declaration is marked by notable moderation. Not a word of hatred for the opposition, not a word of racial ideology, no threat aimed at home or abroad. Hitler says
15   only what they want: the maintenance of the great traditions of our nation, firmness of government instead of eternal wavering, consideration for all the experiences of individual and human life which have proved useful for the welfare of mankind over thousands of years.

    Hindenburg lays wreaths on the graves of the Prussian kings. The old
20   Field Marshal shakes hands with the World War corporal. The corporal makes a deep bow over the hand of the Field Marshal. Cannons thunder over Potsdam – over Germany.

    No one can escape the emotion of the moment. Father too is deeply impressed. Mother has tears in her eyes. I remain silent, ashamed and
25   torn.

Two days later the new Reichstag met in the Kroll Opera House to consider the Enabling Bill, and on this occasion the Nazis revealed a very different image. The Communists (those not already in prison) were refused admittance, whilst the deputies in attendance faced a barrage of intimidation from the ranks of the SA which surrounded the building. A Social Democrat from Bavaria later described the scene:

1 The wide square in front of the Kroll Opera House was crowded with
dark masses of people. We were received with wild choruses: 'We
want the Enabling Act!' Youths with swastikas on their chests eyed us
insolently, blocked our way, in fact made us run the gauntlet, calling us
5 names like 'Centre pig', 'Marxist sow'. The Kroll Opera House was
crawling with armed SA and SS men ... The assembly hall was deco-
rated with swastikas and similar ornaments. When we Social
Democrats had taken our seats on the extreme left, SA and SS men
lined along the walls behind us in a semi-circle. Their expressions boded
10 no good.

However, the Nazis still required a two-thirds majority to pass the
bill and, on the assumption that the Social Democrats would vote
against, they needed the backing of the Centre Party. Hitler thus
promised in his speech of 23 March to respect the rights of the
Catholic Church and to uphold religious and moral values. These
were false promises, which the Centre Party deputies deceived themselves into believing. In the end only the Social Democrats voted
against, and the Enabling Bill was passed by 444 to 94 votes.

Germany had succumbed to what Bracher has called 'legal revolution'.[3] Within the space of a few weeks Hitler had legally dismantled
the Weimar constitution. The way was now open for him to create a
one-party totalitarian dictatorship.

2 *Gleichschaltung*

KEY ISSUES What is meant by *Gleichschaltung?* Which institutions
had been co-ordinated by the end of 1933 and which had not?

The Enabling Act was the constitutional foundation-stone of the
Third Reich. In purely legal terms the Weimar constitution was
never dissolved, but in practice the Enabling Act provided the basis
for creating the arbitrary dictatorship which evolved during 1933.
The intolerance and violence exhibited by the Nazis along the road
to power could now be converted into a tool of government, thus
legally sanctioning the creation of a personal and party dictatorship.
The destruction of Weimar's remaining hallmarks of an open and
liberal society into the Nazi state system is usually referred to as
Gleichschaltung – literally 'bringing into line' or, more commonly, 'co-
ordination'. To some extent *Gleichschaltung* was generated by the
power and freedom now enjoyed by the massed ranks of the SA at
the local level – in effect a 'revolution from below'. But it was also
directed by the Nazi leadership from the political centre in Berlin –
in effect a 'revolution from above'. Together these two political
impulses attempted to 'co-ordinate' as many aspects of German life
as possible along Nazi lines, although differences over the exact

long-term goals of National Socialism laid the basis for future conflict within the Party.

What did *Gleichschaltung* mean in practice? It has been described rather neatly as the 'honeycombing' of German society with Party associations and institutions in a deliberate attempt to Nazify the life of Germany. At first many of these Nazi creations had to live alongside existing bodies, but over the years they gradually replaced them. In this way, much of Germany's cultural, educational and social life was increasingly controlled (see chapter 5). However, in the spring and summer of 1933 it was the 'co-ordination' of Germany's political system which was the real focus of attention, for the continued existence of the federal states, the political parties and an independent labour movement were totally at odds with Nazi political aspirations.

Germany had a very strong tradition of particularism (the devolution of powers away from the centre to the provinces), which since unification had found expression in the continued existence of the previously independent states as largely self-governing federal states within the unitary Reich. Yet, such autonomy stood in marked contrast to Nazi desires to create a fully unified country. Already Nazi activists had exploited the judicial freedom of February–March 1933 to intimidate opponents and to infiltrate federal governments. Indeed, their 'success' rapidly degenerated into violent excesses which seemed beyond the control of Hitler, who called for restraint because he was afraid of losing the support of the conservatives. Thereafter, the situation was given legal basis in April 1933 by two laws which allowed the Nazi-dominated state governments to enact legislation without reference to their *Landtage* (provincial parliaments) and which, secondly, created 18 *Reichstatthalter* (Reich governors) – often the local party *Gauleiters* – with full powers. Centralisation was taken a stage further in January 1934 when the *Landtage* were abolished and the federal governments and governors were subordinated to the Ministry of the Interior. The federal principle of government was as good as dead. Even the Nazi Reich governors existed only 'to execute the will of the supreme leadership of the Reich'.

Germany's trade union movement was powerful by dint of its mass membership and its strong connections with the alternative ideologies of socialism and Catholicism. Back in 1920 it had clearly revealed its industrial muscle when it had successfully ended a right-wing *putsch* by calling a general strike. On the whole, German organised labour was hostile to Nazism and therefore it potentially posed a major threat to the continued stability of the Nazi state. Yet, by May 1933 it was shown to be a spent force. Admittedly the Depression had already quite severely weakened it by reducing membership and lessening the will to resist, but like so many others, the trade union leaders deceived themselves into believing that they could work with the Nazis and thereby preserve a degree of independence and at least the structure of trade unionism. It was hoped that this would allow trade unionism to continue with its social role in the short term, while in the long term providing the framework for development in the post-Nazi era.

However, such self-deception contributed to the labour movement falling prey to a typical piece of Nazi duplicity. The Nazis surprisingly declared 1 May (the traditional day of celebration for international socialist labour) a national holiday, which gave the impression to the trade unions that perhaps there was some scope for co-operation. This proved to be the shortest of illusions. The following day, trade union premises were occupied by the SA and SS and many of the leaders were arrested. All German workers' organisations were then engulfed in DAF (*Deutscher Arbeitsfront* – German Labour Front), which acted more as an instrument of control than as a representative body of workers' interests and concerns. The power of the German trade union movement had been decisively broken. Not only was it politically emasculated, but it had even lost the most fundamental right – to negotiate wages and conditions of work.

Of course, it was inconceivable that *Gleichschaltung* could allow the existence of other political parties. Nazism rejected democracy and any concessions to alternative opinions. Instead, it aspired to establish authoritarian rule within a one-party state. This did not prove difficult to achieve. The Communists had been proscribed since the Reichstag fire, and on 22 June the Social Democrats were officially banned. Yet, all the other major parties adopted a policy of 'self-*Gleichschaltung*' in the course of June and July 1933. Even the Nationalists obligingly opted for self-dissolution. Thus, there was no forum to oppose the decree of 14 July which formally proclaimed the Nazi Party as the only legal political party in Germany.

By mid-1933 the process of *Gleichschaltung* was well-advanced in many spheres of public life in Germany, although it was certainly far from complete. In particular, it had failed to make any impression on the role and influence of the Christian Churches, the Army and big business. This was mainly due to Hitler's determination to regulate the 'revolution from above' and to avoid antagonising such powerful vested interests. However, there were many in the lower ranks of the Party who had contributed to the 'revolution from below' and who now wanted to extend the process of *Gleichschaltung*. It was this internal party conflict which laid the basis for the bloody events of June 1934.

3 The Night of the Long Knives

> **KEY ISSUES** When and why did Hitler decide to crush the SA? Why is the Night of the Long Knives so significant?

In a speech on 6 July 1933 to the Reich governors, Hitler warned of the dangers posed by a permanent state of revolution. He therefore formally declared an end to the revolution and demanded that 'the stream of revolution must be guided into the safe channel of evolution'. He was increasingly concerned that the behaviour of Party activists was running beyond his control and was likely to create embarrassment in his relations with the conservative forces upon whose support he still depended. His speech amounted to an unequivocal demand that the Party accept not only the realities of political compromise, but also the necessity of change from above and not from below.

Hitler's appeal failed to have the desired effect. If anything, it substantiated the fears of many ordinary Nazis that the leadership was prepared to dilute the radical ideology of National Socialism for reasons of political expediency. Such concerns gave rise to demands for the implementation of a second, more radical revolution, which would not hold back from attacking the forces of the German establishment. These calls for further revolutionary action came most strongly from within the ranks of the SA.

The SA tended to represent the populist, anti-capitalist, left wing of the Nazi Party, which to a large extent reflected its more working-class membership. It placed far more emphasis on the socialist elements of the Party programme than Hitler ever did and therefore saw no need to hold back simply for the sake of satisfying conservative social forces. It had played a vital role in the years of struggle by winning the political battle in the streets, and many of its members were embittered by the compromises being made by the regime. They were also disappointed by the limited personal benefits that were accruing from the acquisition of power. Such views were epitomised by the leader of the SA, Ernst Röhm, who called for a genuine 'National Socialist Revolution' and who was increasingly disillusioned by the politics of his old friend Hitler. However, at the very heart of the developing confrontation lay the future role of the SA in the Nazi state. Röhm had no desire to see the SA degenerate into a mere propaganda appendage now that the street-fighting was over. He wanted to integrate the Army and the SA into a people's militia of which he would be the commander. In a private interview in early 1934 with a local Party boss, Rauschning, Röhm gave vent to his feelings and his ideas:

1   Adolf is a swine. He will give us all away. He only associates with the reactionaries now … Getting matey with the East Prussian generals. They're his cronies now … Adolf knows exactly what I want. I've told him often enough. Not a second edition of the old imperial army. Are
5   we revolutionaries or aren't we? … We've got to produce something new, don't you see? A new discipline of organisation. The generals are a lot of old fogeys. They never had a new idea … I'm the nucleus of the new army, don't you see that? Don't you understand that what's coming must be new, fresh and unused? The basis must be revolutionary. You
10 can't inflate it afterwards. You only get the opportunity once to make something new and big that'll help us lift the world off its hinges. But Hitler puts me off with fair words.

Such a plan was anathema to the Army which saw its traditional role and status being directly threatened. Hitler was caught between two powerful but rival forces, either of which could create considerable political difficulties for him. On the one hand, the SA consisted of two and a half million committed Nazis and was led by his oldest political friend. On the other hand, the Army was the one organisation which could unseat him from his position of power. Moreover, it alone possessed the military skills which were vital to the success of his foreign policy aims; however large the SA was, it could never hope to challenge the discipline and professional expertise possessed by the Army.

Political realities dictated that Hitler had to retain the backing of the Army, but in the winter of 1933–4 he was still loath to engineer a show-down with his old friend, Röhm. He tried to appease Röhm by bringing him into the cabinet. He also called a meeting in February between the leaders of the Army, the SA and the SS in an attempt to reach an agreement about the role of each organisation within the Nazi state. However, the tension did not subside. Röhm and the SA resented Hitler's apparent acceptance of the privileged position of the Army, while their own unrestrained actions and ill-discipline only increased the feelings of dissatisfaction amongst the generals.

The developing crisis came to a head in early 1934 when it became apparent that President Hindenburg did not have much longer to live. The implications of his imminent death were profound, for Hitler wanted to assume the presidency without opposition. He certainly did not want a contested election, nor did he have any sympathy for those who desired the restoration of the monarchy. It was the necessity of securing the Army's unqualified backing for his succession to Hindenburg which seems to have forced Hitler's hand. The support of the Army had become the key to his regime's survival in the short term, while in the long term it offered the means to fulfil his ambitions in the field of foreign affairs. Whatever personal loyalty Hitler felt for Röhm and the SA was finally put to one side. The Army desired their elimination and an end to the talk of 'a second revolution' and 'a people's militia'. By agreeing to this, Hitler could gain the favour of the Army generals, secure his personal position and remove an increasingly embarrassing mill-stone from around his neck. Although written evidence of an agreement between Hitler and the Army generals does not exist, it is known that the two parties did meet on the battleship *Deutschland* in April 1934. Also an analysis of the actual events of June 1934 strongly suggests that there was a clear mutual understanding directed against the SA. Furthermore, influential voices within the Nazi Party, in particular Göring and Himmler, were also manoeuvring behind the scenes towards a similar goal in order to further their own ambitions by decisively weakening a powerful rival.

On 30 June 1934, the 'Night of the Long Knives', Hitler eliminated the SA as a political and military force once and for all. Röhm and the main leaders of the SA were shot by members of the SS – although the weapons and transport were provided by the Army. There was no resistance of any substance. In addition, various old scores were settled: Schleicher, the former Chancellor, and Strasser, the leader of the socialist/anti-capitalist wing of the Nazi Party, were both killed. Altogether it is estimated that 400 people were murdered. On 5 July the *Völkischer Beobachter*, the Nazi newspaper, reported on the Reich cabinet meeting held two days earlier:

1   … The Reich Chancellor began by giving a detailed account of the origin and suppression of the high treason plot. The Reich Chancellor stressed that lightning action had been necessary, otherwise many thousands of people would have been in danger of being wiped out.

5   Defence Minister General von Blomberg thanked the Führer in the name of the Cabinet and the Army for his determined and courageous action, by which he had saved the German people from civil war. The Führer had shown greatness as a statesman and a soldier. This had aroused in the hearts of the members of the cabinet and of

10 the whole German people a vow of service, devotion and loyalty in this grave hour.

    The Reich Cabinet then approved a law on measures for the self-defence of the State. Its single paragraph reads: 'The measures taken on 30 June and 1 and 2 July to suppress the acts of high treason are legal,

15 being necessary for the self-defence of the State.'

It would be difficult to overestimate the significance of the Night of the Long Knives. The Army had unequivocally aligned itself behind the Nazi regime, as was shown by Blomberg's public vote of thanks to Hitler on 1 July, while the SA was reduced to the role of a propaganda show-piece and thereafter played no significant role in the political development of the Nazi state. More ominously for the future, it marked the emergence of the SS as the Party's elite institution of terror. Above all, Hitler had secured his own personal political supremacy. On 13 July 1934 he told the Reichstag in a speech:

1   If disaster was to be prevented at all, action must be taken with lightning speed. Only a ruthless and bloody intervention might still perhaps stifle the spread of the revolt … If anyone reproaches me and asks why I did not resort to the regular courts of justice for conviction of the

5 offenders, then all that I can say to him is this: in this hour I was responsible for the fate of the German people, and thereby I became the supreme judge of the German people.

Consequently, when Hindenburg died on 2 August, Hitler was able to merge the offices of Chancellor and President, and also to take on the new official title of Führer. The Nazi regime had been stabilised and the threat of a 'second revolution' had been completely removed.

4 Consolidation or Political Revolution?

> **KEY ISSUE** To what extent did Germany undergo a political revolution in the years 1933–4?

At the Nuremberg Party rally of September 1934 Hitler declared triumphantly and with exultant optimism:

> Just as the world cannot live on wars, so people cannot live on revolutions ... Revolutions have always been rare in Germany ... In the next thousand years there will be no other revolution in Germany.

The word 'revolution' has figured prominently throughout this chapter. Hitler spoke of a 'national revolution', whilst Röhm demanded a 'second revolution'. Likewise, political and historical analysts have written of 'the legal revolution' and the 'revolution from below'. How appropriate is such terminology to describe the events of 1933–4? To what extent had Germany undergone a political revolution?

First of all it is important to recognise that the use of the term 'revolution' is not a prerogative of the political left. It simply means a fundamental change – an overturning of existing conditions. Secondly, it is a dynamic word beloved of politicians and propagandists who use it to stir emotions and to emphasise change. All too often it is used for effect and with scant regard for its real meaning. If Germany did undergo a 'political revolution' in the course of 1933–4, the evidence must indicate that there was a decisive break in the country's line of political development.

At first sight the regime created by the Nazis by the end of 1934 seems to be the antithesis of Germany's immediate political past. However, it should be remembered that the Weimar Republic had ceased to function as an effective democracy well before Hitler became Chancellor. Moreover, the strength of the anti-democratic forces had tormented the young democracy from the very start, so that it was never able to establish strong roots. Yet, even by comparison with pre-1918 Germany, the Nazi regime had wrought fundamental changes: the destruction of the autonomy of the federal states; the intolerance shown towards any kind of political opposition; the reduction of the Reichstag to complete impotence. In all these ways the process of *Gleichschaltung* decisively affected political traditions which had prevailed since the foundation of the *Kaiserreich* in 1871. In this sense it is not unfair to view the events of 1933–4 as a 'political revolution', since the Nazis had turned their backs quite categorically on the federal, liberal and constitutional values which had even permeated an authoritarian regime like that of the *Kaiserreich.*

However, support for the idea of a Nazi political revolution must be tempered by recognising important lines of historical continuity. At the time of Hindenburg's death, major forces within Germany continued to exert an existence independent of the Nazi regime; namely, the Army, big business and the civil service. One might even include the Christian Churches, although they did not carry the same degree of political weight. It was Hitler's willingness to enter into political partnership with these representatives of the old Germany which had encouraged Röhm and the SA to demand a 'second revolution'. The elimination of the power of the SA in the Night of the Long Knives suggests that Hitler's 'national revolution' had just been an attractive anti-Marxist and anti-democratic slogan. In reality this 'revolution' was strictly limited in scope; it involved political compromise and it had refrained from fundamental social and economic change. In this sense one could view the early years of the Nazi regime as merely another political manifestation (albeit the most unpleasant one) of the socio-economic forces which had dominated Germany since 1871.

Summary Diagram
Germany 1933–4: A political revolution?

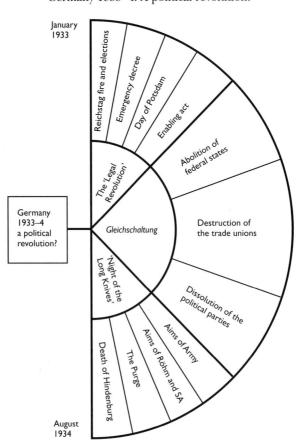

Certainly, such an interpretation would seem to be a fair assessment of the situation up until late 1934. However, the true revolutionary extent of the regime can only be fully assessed by considering the political, social and economic developments that took place in Germany throughout the entire period of the Third Reich. These will be the *foci* of the next few chapters.

References

1 Quoted in W. Carr, *A History of Germany, 1815–1990* (Edward Arnold, 1991) p. 309
2 See H.A. Turner, *German Big Business and the Rise of Hitler* (Oxford, 1985)
3 K.D. Bracher, *The German Dictatorship* (Penguin, 1973) p. 250

Working on Chapter 3

Hopefully, you will have found this chapter relatively straightforward. However, the danger is that you may be tempted to record merely what happened. By all means, use the key dates and the summary diagram as a way of clarifying in your own mind the order of events. But be certain you also make some kind of written assessment of:

a) how significantly each event contributed to the Nazi consolidation of power and
b) how fundamental in reality was the 'Nazi revolution'.

Answering source-based questions on Chapter 3

1. Hitler's 'Appeal to the German People'

Carefully read the boxed extract 'Hitler's Appeal to the German People' on page 40. Answer the following questions:

a) Explain the following references:
   i) 'the November parties' (line 32)
   ii) 'loyal to the command of the Field Marshal' (line 47). (*4 marks*)
b) To whom does Hitler appeal for moral backing for the Nazi regime? (*3 marks*)
c) How does Hitler try to cultivate an image of reasonableness? (*4 marks*)
d) What rhetorical techniques does Hitler use to make his points more forcefully? (*4 marks*)
e) How far would you agree that Hitler's appeal was 'more an attack on the political opposition than a genuine political programme'? (*5 marks*)

2. Nazi Political Methods

Read the extracts describing the Day of Potsdam and the passing of the Enabling Bill on pages 42 and 43. Answer the following questions:

a) Explain the following references
   i) 'Centre pig' (page 43 line 5)
   ii) 'the demagogue' (page 42 line 10). (*2 marks*)
b) Why was Potsdam chosen for the ceremony of 21 March? (*2 marks*)
c) The description of the scene at the Kroll Opera House was written by an avowed opponent of the Nazi regime. In what ways does this affect the value of the evidence to the historian? (*3 marks*)
d) In what ways does Ebermeyer seem to have been won over by the 'Day of Potsdam'? (*4 marks*)
e) The 'Day of Potsdam' and the passage of the Enabling Bill took place within two days of each other. How do you explain the contrast in the ways the Nazis acted on the two occasions? (*4 marks*)

3. The Night of the Long Knives
Carefully read the three extracts on the Night of the Long Knives given on pages 46–48. Answer the following questions:

a) What did Röhm mean when he spoke of the Nazis as revolutionaries? (*3 marks*)
b) From your wider knowledge of Germany in 1934, how much truth do you think there was in Röhm's claim that Hitler 'only associates with the reactionaries now'? (*4 marks*)
c) What is the significance of the law approved on 3 July? (*4 marks*)
d) What are the weaknesses of the account of the Party boss as evidence of Röhm's attitude in 1934? (*3 marks*)
e) With reference to these sources and other evidence known to you, do you believe that there is any substance in the view that the Night of the Long Knives was ordered to prevent an SA revolt against Hitler? (*6 marks*)

Although source-based questions emphasise the skills of analysis and evaluation, there are nearly always marks offered for basic knowledge of the topic. These are often the earlier questions in a series, as can be seen in the above examples. The skill is to write enough to earn yourself high marks, but to recognise that no more than 20 per cent of the overall mark will be ever allocated to such questions. Your answers must, therefore, be precisely focused and concisely written. Above all, you must make certain that you show an understanding of the correct historical context. If all this is done well, it will probably mean writing no more than one or two lines per mark! Thus a good exemplar answer could be along these lines:

1. **a) ii)** The Field Marshal refers to Paul von Hindenburg who was President of Germany from 1925 to 1934. As Hindenburg was previously C-in-C of the Army in the First World War Hitler was keen to present an image of loyalty and respect to the ageing war hero.

4 The Economy of the Third Reich

POINTS TO CONSIDER

This chapter looks at Nazi policies and their impact in the economic sphere. Some of the theories and concepts may seem somewhat daunting, especially for those with little understanding of economics. During your first reading simply try to get clear in your mind the different economic 'phases', whilst also trying to identify some of the positive and negative features of each phase.

KEY DATES

1933	March	Appointment of Schacht as President of the *Reichsbank*.
1934	July	Appointment of Schacht as Minister of Economics.
	Sept	New Plan introduced.
1936	Oct	Four Year Plan established under Göring.
1937	Nov	Resignation of Schacht as Minister of Economics.
1939	Dec	War Economy decrees.
1941	Dec	Rationalisation decree issued by Hitler.
1942	Feb	Appointment of Albert Speer as Minister of Armaments.
1944	Aug	Peak of German munitions production.

1 Nazi Economic Thinking

> **KEY ISSUE** What were the major influences on Nazi economic thinking?

In the years before 1933 Hitler had been careful not to become tied down to the details of an economic policy. For, despite the anti-capitalist sentiments of the 25-point Programme (see page 11), political realities necessitated a certain ambiguity in order to satisfy the different economic interest groups. Hitler even told his cabinet in February 1933 to 'avoid all detailed statements concerning an economic programme of the Government'. However, Hitler was also politically astute enough to realise that his position depended on bringing Germany out of depression and so during 1932 the Nazi leadership had begun to consider more specifically a number of possible approaches to the management of the economy. Firstly, there was the policy of autarky (economic self-sufficiency). This envisaged the creation of a large trading or economic community under the dominating influence of Germany, which could be developed to rival the other great economic powers. It played up ideas of German power and harked back to the expansionist views of some First World War nationalists. Secondly, attention was given to the emerging idea of deficit financing, which found its most obvious expression in the theories of the British economist Keynes. By spending money on public works, it was intended to create jobs which would then act as an artificial stimulus to demand within the economy. Again, such ideas were not wholly objectionable to German right-wing nationalism which had traditionally recognised the role of state intervention in the social and political arena as a means of advancing national aims. Finally, there was the idea of the *Wehrwirtschaft* (defence economy), whereby Germany's peace-time economy was geared to the demands of total war, so as to avoid a repetition of the problems faced during the First World War when a long-drawn-out conflict on two fronts eventually caused economic collapse. Of these three, Hitler identified most closely with the third since it could be related to his long-term political and military aims. However, despite the consideration given to such policies by the Nazi leadership, no coherent plan had emerged by January 1933. Hitler himself had no interest in or understanding of political economy and to a large extent the implementation of economic policy was initially left to bankers and civil servants. From the start then there was a lack of real direction and elements of all three approaches can be detected in the economic history of the Third Reich. This suggests that economic policy tended to be pragmatic and to evolve out of the demands of the situation rather than being the result of careful planning. As one leading historian has stated, 'no single unified economic system prevailed throughout the entire period of the Nazi regime'.[1]

2 Economic Recovery, 1933–6?

> **KEY ISSUES** How did the Nazis approach the task of economic recovery in the short term? How successful was the policy?

In the early years Nazi economic policy was under the control of Hjalmar Schacht, President of the *Reichsbank* (1933–9), and Minister of Economics (1934–7). This reflected the need of the Nazi leadership to work with the powerful forces of big business, for Schacht was already a respected international financier because of his leading role in the creation of the new currency in the wake of the 1923 inflation.

The sheer scale of Germany's economic depression was enormous: mass unemployment; rural poverty; a massive trade slump; and a banking crisis which had led to a collapse in investor confidence. There was no single 'quick fix' solution and under Schacht's guidance and influence a wide range of economic strategies was adopted. Initially, because the German banking system had been so fundamentally weakened, the state increasingly assumed greater responsibility for the control of capital within the economy. It then proceeded to set interest rates at a lower level and to reschedule the large-scale debts of local authorities. Above all, though, it was the major revival in public investment, led for the most part by the state itself, which lay at the heart of economic recovery. Whilst private share issues now required government approval, the state embarked on a large-scale increase in its own expenditure in an effort to stimulate demand and raise national income. This was partly achieved by the indirect methods of lowering tax levels for groups such as farmers and small businesses and of allocating grants of money for house repairs or for the re-hiring of domestic servants. However, of greater significance was the direct expenditure by the state on a range of investment projects. For a long time it was assumed by most historians that rearmament was the main focus, but the figures clearly show that this was not really the case before 1936. By then, the recovery was well advanced. Rather the investment in the first three years was directed towards work creation schemes e.g. reforestation, land reclamation and the creation of the Labour Service; towards motorisation – the policy of developing the vehicle industry and the roads to go with it; and, of vital importance, towards construction – housing and public buildings. The cumulative effect of these policies was to triple public investment between 1933 and 1936 and to increase government expenditure by nearly 70 per cent over the same period. Yet even in 1936, the government deficit was certainly not out of control, since Schacht maintained taxes at a relatively high level and encouraged private savings in state savings banks. Of more public note was the decline in unemployment to 2.1 million in the middle of 1935 from a peak of well over six million, an achievement which drew admiration from both home and abroad. Of course, it must be remembered that all this took place as the world economy began to recover and undoubtedly Schacht was aided by the natural upturn in the business cycle after its nadir in the winter of 1932–3. Nevertheless, it is difficult to believe that such a marked turn-around in investment and employment could have been achieved regardless of Nazi economic policy.

However, this success was also a contributory factor to two economic worries: the fear of rekindling inflation with growing demand, and the emergence of a balance of payments deficit as Germany imported more raw materials without increasing its exports. The problem of inflation never actually materialised because there was still so much slack in the economy and the regime established strict controls over prices and wages – an economic move facilitated by the political act of abolishing the trade unions in May 1933. On the other hand, a balance of payments problem did emerge for the first time in the summer of 1934 and was to recur regularly thereafter.

The balance of payments problem was not merely an economic issue, for it carried with it large-scale political implications. If

Germany was so short of foreign exchange, which sector of the economy was to have priority in spending the money? The Economics Minister, Schmitt, wanted to reduce unemployment further by manufacturing more consumer goods for public consumption. However, powerful voices in the armed forces and big business were already demanding more resources for the embryonic rearmament programme. Hitler could not ignore such pressure – especially as this economic problem coincided with the political dilemma over the SA (see page 47). Consequently, Schmitt's policy was rejected and he was removed, thereby allowing Schacht to combine the offices of Minister of Economics and President of the *Reichsbank*. By a law of 3 July, he was given dictatorial powers over the economy, which he then used to introduce the 'New Plan' of September 1934. This provided for a comprehensive control by the government of all aspects of trade and currency exchange. In this way the government set the priorities. As a result, for example, in 1934 imports of raw cotton and wool were substantially cut in order to satisfy the import demands of heavy industry. Schacht also tried to promote trade and save foreign exchange by signing bilateral trade treaties, especially with the countries of south-east Europe and South America. These often took the form of straightforward barter agreements (thus avoiding the necessity of formal currency exchange). Alternatively, Germany agreed to purchase raw materials from such countries on the condition that the marks could only be used to buy back German goods (at one time it is estimated that the German mark had 237 different values depending on the country and the circumstances!). In this way Germany began to exert a powerful economic influence over the Balkans long before it obtained military and political control.

Schacht was not a Nazi, but his proven economic skills earned him respect both in and outside the Party and it was he who laid the foundations for economic recovery. By mid-1936 unemployment had fallen to 1.5 million; industrial production had increased by 60 per cent since 1933; and GNP had grown over the same period in real terms by 40 per cent. However, such successes masked fundamental structural weaknesses which came to a head in the second half of 1936 over the future direction of the German economy.

3 The Four Year Plan – A War Economy in Peace-Time?

KEY ISSUES What was the main purpose of the Four Year Plan? Why did it lead to Schacht's resignation? What was the condition of the German economy at the time of the outbreak of war in September 1939?

In many respects, as Schacht himself was only too aware, he had merely hidden the balance of payments problem by a series of clever financial tricks. And, despite his apparent sympathy for deficit financing, Schacht believed that the combination of a budget deficit and a balance of payments deficit could not be maintained indefinitely. In early 1936 it became clear to him that, as the demands for rearmament and consumption increased, the German balance of payments would go deeply into the red. He therefore suggested a reduction in arms expenditure in order to increase the production of industrial exports which at least could be sold so as to earn foreign exchange. Such a solution had its adherents, especially in the export-oriented industries, but it was unacceptable to the armed forces and to the Nazi leadership. In August 1936 Hitler produced the following memorandum:

1   ...The development of our military capacity is to be effected through the new Army. The extent of the military development of our resources cannot be too large, nor its pace too swift....If we do not succeed in bringing the German Army as rapidly as possible to the rank
5 of premier Army in the world so far as its training, raising of units, armaments and above all its spiritual education also is concerned, then Germany will be lost.

    Parallel with the military and political rearmament and mobilisation of our nation must go its economic rearmament and mobilisation, and
10 this must be effected in the same tempo, with the same determination, and if need be with the same ruthlessness as well. In future the interests of individual gentlemen can no longer play any part in these matters. There is only one interest, the interest of the nation; only one view, the bringing to the point of political and economic self-sufficiency.
15   For this purpose foreign exchange must be saved in all those areas where our needs can be satisfied by German production.

    Accordingly, German fuel production must now be stepped up with the utmost speed and brought to final completion.

    The mass production of synthetic rubber must also be organised and
20 achieved with the same urgency.

    The question of the cost of producing these raw materials is also quite irrelevant.

The politico-economic crisis of 1936 was resolved by the introduction of the Four Year Plan under the control of Hermann Göring in October of that year. Its fundamental aim was to make the German armed forces and economy ready for war within four years. In order to achieve this, the Plan highlighted four objectives: an increase in agricultural production; the retraining of key sectors of the labour force; government regulation of imports and exports to satisfy strategic priorities; and, above all, the achievement of self-sufficiency in raw materials, such as oil, rubber and metals – if necessary by the development of *ersatz* (synthetic) substitutes. Such a programme marked an important turning-point in the Nazi regime. Nazi control over industry became much tighter, and Schacht found his influence on the wane, as he himself described in his book written in 1949:

1 ...Göring set out, with all the folly and incompetence of the amateur, to carry out the programme of economic self-sufficiency, or autarky, envisaged in the Four Year Plan. He exploited the plenary powers Hitler had given him as chief of the Four Year Plan operations in order to
5 extend his own influence over economic policy, which he did not find difficult, since he was now, of course, in a position to place really large contracts ... On December 17th 1936, Göring informed a meeting of big industrialists that it was no longer a question of producing economically, but simply of producing. And as far as getting hold of foreign
10 exchange was concerned it was quite immaterial whether the provisions of the law were complied with or not ... Göring's policy of recklessly exploiting Germany's economic substance necessarily brought me into more and more acute conflict with him, and for his part he exploited his powers, with Hitler and the Party behind him, to counter
15 my activity as Minister of Economics to an ever-increasing extent.

Schacht eventually resigned in November 1937 and was replaced by the subservient Walther Funk, though from this time Göring himself became the real economic dictator. The success of the Plan was mixed. On the one hand, production of a number of key materials, such as aluminium and explosives, had expanded greatly, while in others it had grown at a respectable rate. On the other hand, it fell a long way short of the targets in the vital commodities of rubber and oil, whilst arms production never reached the levels desired by the armed forces and Hitler. All in all, the Four Year Plan had succeeded in the sense that Germany's reliance on imports had not deteriorated any further, but this still meant that when war did break out Germany was dependent on foreign supplies for one-third of its raw materials.

The research of B.H. Klein in the 1950s led him to argue that this partial economic mobilisation was actually a deliberate policy allied to the military strategy of *Blitzkrieg*. In his view, Hitler and the armed forces recognised Germany's precarious position over raw materials, and consequently developed the strategy of short wars, which would avoid the economic strain of 'total war' This also had the political advantage of not reducing the production of consumer goods excessively. Klein argued that pre-1939 civilian consumption remained comfortable and that the 'the scale of Germany's economic mobilisation for war was quite modest'. Indeed, he claimed, it was not until after the defeat at Stalingrad in the winter of 1942–3 that full economic mobilisation began in earnest.[2]

Klein's basic thesis has proved to be very influential, although it was somewhat modified in the mid-1960s by Milward. He accepted that *Blitzkrieg* was meant to avoid total war, but he also pointed out that 'no nation had ever previously spent so vast a sum on preparations for war'. Moreover, he suggested that it was the German failure to take Moscow at the end of 1941 that was the real economic turning-point. By spring 1942 the German economic machine was ready for the war of attrition.[3]

Such interpretations have now begun to be questioned. Prompted by the views of diplomatic historians, who see Hitler stumbling unintentionally into a major European war in September 1939, economic historians have started to revise their opinions about the direction and state of the German economy. Overy has argued forcefully that from the start Hitler envisaged a great conflict for world power and that this necessitated the transformation of the economy to the demands of total war.[4] However, his preparations for this kind of war were not intended to be finished until 1943. The war with Poland in 1939 was meant to be a local war, which Hitler wrongly believed would not involve Britain and France. The premature outbreak of continental conflict inevitably found the German economy only partially mobilised. However, in Overy's opinion, the underlying principles of Nazi economic policy were already abundantly clear. The German economy from 1936 had been unashamedly directed towards war preparation, so that two-thirds of all German investment went into war-related projects. Full employment was achieved, but over a quarter of the work-force was involved in rearmament. Levels of government expenditure more than doubled in the same period with the result that the government debt increased likewise. In the last full year of peace 17 per cent of Germany's GNP went on military expenditure (compared to 8 per cent in Britain and 10 per cent in the USA). According to such a view then, the German economy by 1939 was already an economy dominated by the preparations for war, though this did not yet amount to the full-scale mobilisation required of total war, since total war was not envisaged until about 1943. In a thought-provoking conclusion Overy suggests:

> 1 ... If war had been postponed until 1943–5 as Hitler had hoped, then Germany would have been much better prepared, and would also have had rockets, jet aircraft, inter-continental bombers, perhaps even atomic weapons. Though Britain and France did not know it, declaring
> 5 war in 1939 prevented Germany from becoming the super-power Hitler wanted. The drive for total war became instead *Blitzkrieg* by default.[5]

Not surprisingly, such a fundamental reorientation of the German economy created added political and economic pressures, as is revealed in a telling contemporary analysis by a member of the SPD:

> 1 The Nazis try to persuade the nation that the problem of economic constraints is nothing but a foreign exchange problem; in reality it is a problem of the capacity of the economy and of the nation's willingness to make sacrifices. This problem has two aspects; the problem of

5 economic resources, of the maximum level of production and the minimum level of consumption; and the problem of money, of financial constraints. What the superficial observer notices is the constricting effect of the foreign exchange shortage with which Germany continually has to cope. If the German people do not get enough butter and fats, if they
10 have to stuff their stomachs with inferior bread, if the objects of daily use have to be made of dubious *ersatz* materials then it seems at first sight – and that is what the Nazis try to persuade the people – as if the blame for that lies in Germany's dependence on foreign countries, which finds expression in the shortage of foreign exchange.
15 This superficial view makes the false theory of autarky popular in Germany.

Such contradictions within the German economy have led some historians to go as far as to suggest that by 1939 the situation was so serious that Hitler embarked on war as the only way out of Germany's domestic economic dilemma. This seems unlikely. There really was no need to rush into war when the 'smash and grab' policy of 1938–9 had proved to be so effective (see pages 125–130). Germany found itself at war in September 1939 because of diplomatic miscalculation. Its economy was still a long way short of being fully mobilised, but it was certainly on more of a war-footing than Britain or France – the question now was whether Germany could complete the economic mobilisation and thereby effect military victory.

4 The Failure to Mobilise the Economy, 1939–41

> **KEY ISSUE** What were the limitations of Germany's economic
> mobilisation in the early years of the war?

The string of military successes achieved by the German armed forces with their use of *Blitzkrieg* strategy up to December 1941 won Hitler and the regime valuable popular support. Moreover, it gave the impression of an economy which had not been unduly strained by the rigours of war – a fact which Klein and Milward used to substantiate their claim that the Nazis deliberately developed and then pursued the complementary economic and military policies of *Blitzkrieg* and partial economic mobilisation until 1942 or 1943. Such a view, however attractive, does not actually square with either Nazi intentions or the economic statistics. Firstly, Hitler himself was determined to avoid the problems faced by Germany in the First World War and to fight the coming war with an economy thoroughly prepared for a major and perhaps extended conflict. To this end a series of war economy decrees was issued by Hitler in December 1939 outlining vast programmes for every possible aspect of war production which went well beyond the demands of *Blitzkrieg* and a limited war. In real and percentage terms, German military expenditure doubled between 1939 and 1941 (though that of Britain trebled). It is also the case that food rationing was introduced from the very start of the war and that the German labour force was rapidly mobilised for war, so that by the summer of 1941 55 per cent of the work force was involved in war-related projects – a figure which then only crept up to a high-point of 61 per cent by 1944. In this light it is hardly surprising that the first two years of war also witnessed a 20 per cent decline in civilian consumption.

However, despite the intent of wholesale mobilisation the actual results, in terms of armaments production, remained disappointingly low. Admittedly, there was a marked increase in the number of submarines, but amazingly Germany's air-force had only increased from 8,290 in 1939 to 10,780 in 1941 while in Britain over the same period the number of aircraft had trebled to 20,100. Likewise, Hitler was astonished to learn when drawing up plans for the invasion of the USSR that the Germans' armoured strength totalled only 3,500 tanks which was just 800 more than for the invasion of the West. It seems that despite the projected image of German order and purposefulness, the actual mobilisation of the German economy was marred by inefficiency and poor co-ordination. The pressures resulting from the premature outbreak of war created problems since many of the major projects were not due to be ready until 1942–3, and so, at first, there was undoubtedly confusion between short-term needs and long-term plans. Nevertheless, this should not have been an insuperable barrier if only a clear and authoritative central control had been established over the economy. Instead, a host of different agencies all continued to function in their own way and often in a fashion which put them at odds with each other. So, although there was a Ministry of Armaments, it existed alongside three other interested governmental ministries, those of Economics, Finance and Labour. In addition, there was the Office of the Four Year Plan and various military and SS bodies. The armed forces, in particular, were determined to have their way over the development of munitions with the best specifications possible and as a result the drive for quality was pursued at the expense of quantity. The consequence of all this was that after two years of war and with the armed forces advancing into the USSR Germany's economic mobilisation for total war just had not achieved the expected levels of armaments production.

5 Total War?

> **KEY ISSUE** How effectively did the German economy respond to the demands of 'total war'?

By the end of 1941 Germany was at war with Britain, the USSR and the USA and yet its armaments production remained inferior to that of Britain. Preparations for a new approach had begun in the autumn of 1941 and Hitler had issued a 'Rationalisation Decree' in December of that year, but it was the appointment of Albert Speer as Minister of Armaments in February 1942 which marked the real turning point. Speer had previously been the Führer's personal architect and he enjoyed excellent relations with Hitler. He now used the Führer's authority to cut through the myriad of interests and to implement his programme of 'industrial self-responsibility'. The controls and constraints placed upon business, in order to subject it to Nazi wishes, were relaxed. In their place there was established in April 1942 a Central Planning Board, which was in turn supported by a number of committees, each representing one vital sector of the economy. This gave the industrialists a considerable degree of freedom, whilst ensuring that Speer as the director of Central Planning was able to maintain overall control of the war economy. Speer also sought to encourage industrialists and engineers to join his ministerial team and at the same time, wherever possible, to exclude military personnel from the production process.

Speer was what would now be called a 'technocrat'. He simply co-ordinated and rationalised the process of war production and thereby more effectively exploited the potential of Germany's resources and labour force. Over the next two years, a quite remarkable transformation took place. Total arms production increased by 59 per cent during the first six months alone and by the second half of 1944, when German war production peaked, there had been more than a threefold increase since early 1942.

Nevertheless, Speer's economic successes should not disguise the fact that Germany actually had the capacity to produce even more and could have achieved a level of output close to that of the USSR or the USA. He was not always able to counter the power of the Party *Gauleiters* at a local level and the economic agencies of the SS remained a law unto themselves, especially in the conquered lands. Indeed, although the occupied territories of the Third Reich were well and truly plundered, they were not exploited in an economically efficient fashion. Above all, though, from 1943 Speer could not reverse the detrimental effects of Anglo-American bombing. After the war 'blanket bombing' by the Allies was condemned on moral grounds and its effectiveness denied – indeed, critics pointed to Speer's production figures as proof that the strategy had failed to break the German war economy. However, it is probably more accurate to say that the effects of bombing prevented Germany from increasing its levels of arms production even higher. In other words, if it had not been for the destruction, the breakdown in communications and the need to divert available resources towards the construction of anti-aircraft installations and underground industrial sites, which were all the result of bombing, then Germany could well have achieved a total war economy. As it was, German arms production peaked in August 1944 at a level well below its full potential. In the end, the Nazi economy had proved incapable of rising to the demands of total war and the cost of that failure was all too clearly to be seen in the ruins and economic collapse of 1945.

References

1 A. Schweitzer, *Big Business in the Third Reich* (New York, 1972) p. 1
2 See B.H. Klein, *Germany's Economic Preparations for War* (Harvard, 1959)
3 See A.S. Milward, *The German Economy at War* (London, 1965)
4 See R.J. Overy, *The Nazi Economic Recovery, 1932–38* 2nd ed. (Cambridge, 1996)
5 R.J. Overy, 'Did Hitler Want Total War?' in *History Sixth* No. 4 1989 p. 30

Summary Diagram
The strengths and weaknesses of the Nazi economy

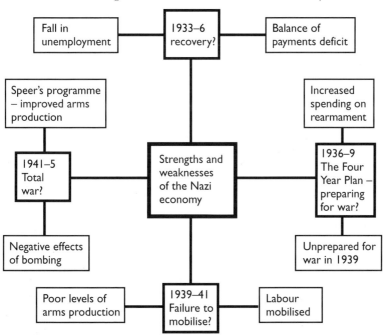

Working on Chapter 4

The content of this chapter is integral to your understanding of many other aspects of Nazi Germany. So it is important that you feel comfortable with the topic before moving on to chapters 5, 6 and 7, even if you finally decide to refrain from answering specific questions on the Nazi economy. To this end you should at least use the summary diagram as a framework for jotting down the economic successes and failures during each phase. Also try to make a brief assessment of whether the balance lies on the success or the failure side. If you want to take the topic further, you will need to develop the above approach more fully by revisiting the text and noting down a lot more of the supporting detail. Answering the source-based questions will also increase your understanding of the topic.

Answering source-based questions on Chapter 4

Read the extracts from Hitler's memo (page 57), Schacht's memoirs (page 58) and the SPD analysis (pages 59–60). Answer the following questions.

a) Explain:
  i) 'Göring exploited the plenary powers Hitler had given him.' (page 58 line 3)
  ii) 'dubious *ersatz* materials' (page 60 line 11). (*4 marks*)
b) What were the main aims of the Four Year Plan? (*5 marks*)
c) i) How far does Schacht support the view expressed by the SPD analysis about the effectiveness of Nazi economic policy? (*4 marks*)
  ii) How reliable are these two documents as evidence of the condition of the German economy under the Nazis? (*4 marks*)
d) Do these documents, and other evidence known to you, support the assertion that 'Nazi economic policy made a war of conquest inevitable'? (*8 marks*)

Many sets of source-based questions include one question which will involve the ability to make comparisons between documents. There are several pieces of advice to bear in mind. Firstly, there is a great danger that you end up simply working your way through the whole of both documents, when usually there is a particular point of focus provided in the wording of the question which you should be concentrating on. In question c) i) above, that focus is the issue of 'effectiveness'. Secondly, it is a good idea to take one document first and to look for individual points which can then act as a kind of 'benchmark' for the second document. You should be aiming to highlight points of similarity, difference and omission in both content and style. This use of a 'bench-mark' is even more important if the question involves three documents and you are asked to assess one document against the other two.

The Social and Racial Impact of the Third Reich

POINTS TO CONSIDER

This chapter covers a very broad range of topics and, unlike in most other chapters, each of sections 2 to 7 could be viewed as a self-contained unit. As you read the chapter for the first time try to assess what was changed and what remained unchanged within German society.

KEY DATES

1933	**May**	The burning of the books.
		Creation of German Labour Front.
	July	Concordat signed with the Papacy.
1934		Reich Ministry of Education created: control of education wrested from *Länder*.
1935	**Sept**	Nuremberg Race Laws promulgated.
1937		Papal encyclical issued, *Mit Brennender Sorge*.
1938		*Kristallnacht*: anti-Jewish pogrom.
1942		Wannsee Conference: 'Final Solution' to the Jewish problem agreed on.

1 Nazi Views on Society

> **KEY ISSUE** What did the Nazis mean by the creation of a *Volksgemeinschaft*?

Hitler always claimed that National Socialism was more than just a political party. It was a movement and an ideology that aimed to exercise power so as to transform German society. It recoiled against the prevailing values of liberal individualism and socialist class warfare, and in their place it upheld the concept of *Volksgemeinschaft*, or people's community. By trying to bridge class and social divisions this idea had become an important element in Nazism's attempt to achieve a broad-based appeal in the elections of 1930–32 as Germany's first genuine people's party (see also page 13). However, once in power, it meant the propagation of Nazi social and racial theories in a deliberate attempt to integrate the disparate elements; in effect to remodel German society so that existing class, religious or regional identities would be replaced by a new sense of 'national' community based upon Nazi ideas of race and struggle. Of course, this would exclude certain groups such as Jews, Communists and social outcasts, like alcoholics, but in general membership of the *Volksgemeinschaft* was open to all who were prepared to accept the constraints of Nazi authoritarianism. Although it is difficult to go beyond these rather nebulous intimations of Nazi social ideology, it should be clear nevertheless that the fundamental historical question raised by the idea of the *Volksgemeinschaft* is whether German society was fundamentally changed during the life of the Third Reich.

2 Material Conditions

KEY ISSUE Who benefited from the Nazi regime?

On a very general level the revival of the economy (in conjunction with Hitler's diplomatic successes) contributed greatly to the German people's acceptance, or at least tolerance, of the regime. In the pre-war years it really did seem to many Germans as if the Nazis had pulled their country out of the economic quagmire. However, in material terms the effects varied considerably from one class to another.

For the industrial working class there were the positive benefits of regular work, stable rents, and recreational provision organised by the Nazi KDF (*Kraft durch Freude* – Strength through Joy), which provided very real opportunities to millions of workers – cultural visits, sports facilities and holiday travel. However, against these advantages must be set the loss of industrial bargaining rights and the demands placed on workers by management and by the government, which intervened to control pay increases and to limit workers' freedom of movement. From May 1933 workers had no real option but to join the DAF (*Deutsche Arbeitsfront* – German Labour Front) and to accept its stipulations on working conditions. The analysis of workers' wages has proved to be a highly complicated issue, mainly because there are so many variables to take into account, such as age, occupation and geographical location. However, the average worker's real wages (the actual purchasing power after taking into account the inflation rate) only rose above 1929 levels in 1938. Moreover, the average working week had increased from 43 hours in 1933 to 47 hours in 1939. Despite all the complications, it is clear that this generalised picture disguises one definite point of differentiation: the best gains were made by those in industries associated with the rearmament boom, while those in consumer goods struggled to maintain their real incomes.

The farming community had been attracted to the Nazi cause by the promise of economic aid and by the apparent sympathy of National Socialism for its role in society. The Nazi ideology of 'Blood and Soil' portrayed the peasantry as racially the purest element of the *Volk*, and as representative of those traditional values which were being lost in the amorphous urban society of industrial Germany. Yet, economic realities meant that in practice the impact of Nazi policy was rather mixed. Certainly, a substantial number of farm debts were written off, and all farmers benefited from an increase in prices betweeen 1933 and 1936. However, the Reich Food Estate, established in 1933, controlled every aspect of agricultural production and consumption, and its bureaucratic meddling became the focus of much resentment (each hen, it was stipulated, had to lay 65 eggs per year!). Even the *Reich Entailed Farm Law* of 1933, which gave security of tenure to the occupiers of medium-sized farms between 7.5 and 125 hectares, was resented. This was because, since it forbade the division of farms, farmers faced a very real problem in providing a future for more than one of their children. Indeed, by the late 1930s, despite the regime's desire to increase agricultural production, it was clear that there had been a significant drift of workers to the towns where wages were higher. German agriculture just did not have the economic power to compete with other sectors of the economy and, as there were limits to Nazi interventionism and economic regulation, it faced a severe shortage of labour.

Another social class which expected to benefit from the Nazi regime was the *Mittelstand* – the class of small-scale retailers and self-employed artisans. Yet, its position continued to decline under the Nazis, since only a very limited attempt was made to implement the electoral promises. The harsh commercial realities of the 1930s, together with the Nazi preference for big business, whose support was required for rearmament, simply perpetuated the trend of relative economic decline which went back to the beginnings of Germany's industrialisation. In 1933 20 per cent of the owners of *Mittelstand* businesses were under 30 years old and 14 per cent over 60. By 1939 the corresponding figures were 10 per cent and 19 per cent. The truth is that the *Mittelstand* found itself squeezed out as a result of changing economic conditions which were completely beyond its control and about which the Nazi government was not prepared to regulate now that it needed to maintain the sympathies of those economic interest groups involved in arms production.

The role of big business will be considered in more depth in the next chapter, but for the moment suffice it to say that generally it benefited from the economic programme of the Nazis. Despite a range of government controls, the financial gains were impressive. The value of German industry steadily increased, as shown by the rise in the share index from 41 points in 1932 to 106 in 1940, whilst annual dividends to investors grew from an average 2.83 per cent to 6.60 per cent over the same period. Such growth was also reflected in the improved salaries of management – from an average 3,700RM in 1934 to 5,420RM in 1938.

3 Anti-Semitism: from Persecution to Extermination

KEY ISSUES How was it possible for the state apparatus of a civilised nation to effect such a policy? To what extent was this policy a result of the long-cherished aim of Hitler alone?

At the very centre of Nazi social policy was the issue of race, and by extension, anti-Semitism. Hitler's obsessive hatred of the Jews was perhaps the most dominant and consistent theme of his political career. The translation of such ideas into actual policy was to lead to economic boycotts, racial laws, government-inspired violence and pogroms, and finally, to the obscenities of mass-shootings and the gas-chambers. This is not the place for a detailed factual account of such episodes, although the table on page 69 does give a brief chronology. Rather, it is more important to think about the key issues raised by the Nazi racial policy, which eventually culminated in geno-cide – or, as it has more commonly become known, 'the Holocaust'. For historians, such questions pose immense problems. The detached rational objectivity required of historical analysis is exceedingly difficult to achieve when the subject is of itself so emotive, so fantastic and in many respects so irrational. And yet, such questions cannot be ignored.

There is a long tradition of anti-Semitism in European history. It was not the preserve of the Nazis, and it certainly has never been just a purely German phenomenon. It was rooted in the religious hostility of Christendom towards the Jews (as the murderers of Jesus) which can be traced back many centuries. Yet, there emerged in Germany in the course of the nineteenth century a more clearly defined anti-Semitism, which was based upon racism and social resentment. By 1900 a number of specifically anti-Semitic political parties were winning seats in the Reichstag and, although they were comparatively few, the successes illustrate that anti-Semitic ideas were becoming more prevalent and generally more respectable. Some historians have seen this anti-Semitism as a by-product of the nationalist passions stirred up by unification and the emergence of Germany as a world power. However, it should be remembered that a similar development had also taken place in German-speaking Austria, and there the political situation was very different.

In reality, the emergence of political anti-Semitism was a response to intellectual developments and changing sociological conditions. The Jews became an easy scapegoat for the discontent and disorientation felt by many people as rapid industrialisation and urbanisation took place. The Jewish community was easily identifiable because of its different traditions, and became the focus of envy because it was viewed as privileged. In 1933, for example, although Jews comprised

Chronology of Jewish Persecution, 1933–45

1933	1 April	First official boycott of Jewish shops and professions.
	7 April	Law for the Restoration of the Professional Civil Service excluded Jews from government jobs.
1934		Jews prohibited from the professions.
1935	15 September	Nuremberg Race Laws:
		1) Reich Citizenship Act. 'A citizen of the Reich is that subject only who is of German or kindred blood.'
		2) Law for the Protection of German Blood and German Honour. Marriages between Jews and German citizens forbidden. Extra-marital relations between Jews and German citizens forbidden.
1936	Summer	Decline in anti-Semitic campaign because of Berlin Olympics.
1937		Intensification of Aryanisation programme in commerce and professions.
1938	28 October	Expulsion of 17,000 Polish Jews resident in Germany.
	7 November	Assassination of Ernst von Rath, a German diplomat in Paris, by Herschel Grünspan, a Jew.
	9 November	*Kristallnacht* (Crystal Night), pogrom throughout Germany. Destruction of Jewish shops, homes and synagogues. 100 Jews killed and 20,000 sent to concentration camps.
	15 November	Expulsion of Jewish pupils from schools.
	3 December	Compulsory closure and sale of all Jewish businesses.
1939	30 April	Confiscation of all Jewish valuables.
	1 September	Introduction of curfew for Jews.
1940		First deportations of Jews from certain German provinces.
1941	June	*Einsatzgruppen* (Action squads) of SS moved into the USSR behind the advancing armies to round up and kill Jews.
1941	1 September	All Jews forced to wear the Yellow Star of David.
1942	20 January	Wannsee Conference. Various government and Party agencies agreed on the 'Final Solution' to the Jewish problem.
	Spring	Extermination facilities set up at Auschwitz, Majdanek and Treblinka.
1943	February	Destruction of Warsaw Ghetto.
	Summer	Transportation of Jews from all over German-occupied Europe to death camps began, resulting in the death of approximately 6 million Jews.
1945	26 January	Liberation of Auschwitz by Soviet troops.

less than 1 per cent of the German population, they composed more than 16 per cent of lawyers, 10 per cent of doctors and 5 per cent of editors and writers. In the late nineteenth century anti-Semitism also began to be presented in a more intellectual vein by the application of racial theories of Social Darwinism. According to such thinking, nations were like animals and only by struggling and fighting could they hope to survive. In this way, an aura of intellectual respectability was given to those anti-Semites who portrayed the Jews as an 'inferior' or 'parasitic' race. One leading historian of Nazi Germany has claimed that by 1914, 'in the form of a basic dislike of the Jews and of what they were felt to represent, it [anti-Semitism] had succeeded in permeating broad sections of German society from the Kaiser down to the lower middle class. Ominously, it was particularly strongly entrenched within the academic community, thereby influencing the next generation.'[1]

It was in such an environment that Hitler's anti-Semitism developed. He was the product, not the creator, of a society which was permeated by such prejudices. However, it would be inaccurate to dismiss Hitler as just another anti-Semite. Hitler's hatred of Jews was obsessive and vindictive, and it shaped much of his political philosophy. Without his personal commitment to attack the Jews and without his charismatic skills as a political leader, it seems unlikely that anti-Semitism could have become such an integral part of the Nazi movement. That he was able to do this can only be explained by the unique circumstances of post-war Germany: the self-deception of the 'stab in the back'; the humiliation of Versailles; the political weakness of the Weimar Republic; and the extreme socio-economic problems of 1918–23 and 1929–33. In such a situation, Hitler was able to exploit latent hostility towards the Jews and turn it into a radical doctrine of hatred.

However, the appointment of an anti-Semite as Chancellor, even if he did enjoy 37.3 per cent of the popular vote, cannot on its own explain the events of 1933–45. Indeed, in a 1934 survey into the reasons why people joined the Nazis, over 60 per cent did not even mention anti-Semitism. How then was it possible to translate the rhetoric of Nazi anti-Semitism into the brutal policy of 1933–45?

At first the Nazi approach was gradualist. The early moves against the Jews gave no suggestion of the end result. Indeed, for some Germans the boycotts and discriminatory legislation were no more than the Jews deserved. For the more liberally-minded, who found such action offensive, there was the practical problem of how to show opposition and to offer resistance. Once the apparatus of dictatorship was well-established by the end of 1934, the futility of opposition was apparent to most people. Feelings of hopelessness were increasingly superseded by those of fear. To show sympathy or to protect the Jews was to risk one's own freedom or one's own life. It was an unenviable dilemma. Another explanation of popular attitudes is offered by Melita Maschmann in her memoirs:

1   I had learned from the example of my parents that one could have anti-
Semitic opinions without this interfering in one's personal relations
with individual Jews. There may be a vestige of tolerance in this attitude,
but it is really just this confusion which I blame for the fact that I later
5 contrived to dedicate body and soul to an inhuman political system,
without this giving me doubts about my own individual decency. In
preaching that all the misery of the nations was due to the Jews or that
the Jewish spirit was seditious and Jewish blood corrupting, I was not
compelled to think of you or old Herr Lewy or Rosel Cohn: I thought
10 only of the bogy-man, 'The Jew'. And when I heard that the Jews were
being driven from their professions and homes and imprisoned in ghet-
tos, the points switched automatically in my mind to steer me round
the thought that such a fate could also overtake you or old Lewy. It was
only *the* Jew who was being persecuted and 'made harmless'.

As for the Jewish community itself, the persecution did lead to the
emigration of nearly 150,000 people (nearly 30 per cent of the 1933
Jewish population) between 1933 and 1938. But the majority preferred to take their chance in Germany, rather than lose their homes
and possessions by leaving.

It is of course the inconceivable nature of events after 1939 which
partially explain why the Holocaust was possible. Who in 1939 could
have predicted the scenario of the next six years? The suggestion that
millions would be systematically exterminated would have defied
belief. It is an event in modern European history which even now is
almost beyond rational comprehension. For those who lived in occupied Europe it was easier and more comfortable to dismiss the
rumours as gross and macabre exaggerations – the result of war-time
gossip and Allied propaganda.

Yet, the unbelievable did happen, and it required not only the pas-
sivity of the 'innocent' majority but also the actions of a 'criminal'
minority. In Germany the moral dimension has helped to make this
historical debate a particularly lively one. Indeed, this aspect of its
past remains central to the dilemma of modern Germany's identity as
a nation. Rather controversially, the American historian Daniel
Goldhagen has recently suggested in his book *Hitler's Willing
Executioners* that the Holocaust was possible because so many ordinary
Germans were prepared to participate in the Third Reich's darkest
deed.[2] This is explained according to Goldhagen by the fact that
within German culture there had developed a virulent and violent
eliminationist variant of anti-Semitism. Such a view has resurrected
the old controversy of 'collective national guilt and shame' though in
academic circles the book has not been generally well-received.
Goldhagen has been condemned for selecting his evidence to prove
his thesis and thereby failing to recognise other overtly anti-Semitic
cultures in pre-1933 Europe, as well as ignoring the role of many non-
Germans in the murder of the Jews.

Of course, there is no denying that there were some real psychopaths and sadists (as in any society) who enjoyed the blood-letting. And there were also the Party fanatics, such as Heydrich, Eichmann and Himmler, who genuinely believed in the righteousness of the 'Final Solution'. In October 1943 Himmler spoke to a group of SS commanders in occupied Poland:

1   I want to speak here before you in all openness about a very delicate subject. Among us it should be talked about quite openly, but despite this we shall never talk about it in public. I mean the evacuation of the Jews, the extermination of the Jewish people. This is one of those things
5   that one says easily enough. 'The Jewish people will be exterminated,' says many a party comrade. 'OK – stands in the programme – elimination of Jews – extermination – we'll do it' ... Of all the people that talk that way, none has seen it happen, none has been through it. Most of you know what it means when 100 corpses are lying together, when
10   500 are lying there, or when 1,000 are lying there. To have seen that through and while doing so – leaving aside exceptions owing to human weakness – to have maintained our integrity, that has made us hard. This is an unwritten and never-to-be written page of glory in our history.

Equally, there were those who were prepared to implement policy and to accept their orders almost without question whilst deluding themselves that what they were doing was part of a higher mission. In his autobiography, completed shortly before his execution, Rudolf Höss, the commandant at Auschwitz, wrote:

1   I had to appear cold and indifferent to events which must have wrung the heart of anyone possessed of human feelings ... I had to watch coldly while the mothers with laughing or crying children went to the gas-chambers ... I had to see everything. I had to watch hour by hour,
5   by night and by day, the burning and the removal of the bodies, the extraction of the teeth, the cutting of the hair, the whole grisly business ... I had to do all this, because I was the one to whom everyone looked, because I had to show them all that I did not merely issue the orders and make the regulations but was also prepared to be present at what-
10   ever task I had assigned to my subordinates ... In the face of such grim considerations I was forced to bury all human considerations as deeply as possible ... I had to observe everything with a cold indifference ... In Auschwitz, I truly had no reason to complain that I was bored ... I had only one end in view, to drive everyone and everything forward, so that
15   I could accomplish the measures laid down ... Every German had to commit himself heart and soul, so that we might win the war ... By the will of the *Reichsführer* SS, Auschwitz became the greatest human extermination centre of all time.

It is a poignant and revealing insight into a man who admitted responsibility for the death of at least 1,250,000 human beings.

However, the reality is that for the majority of the young men in the action squads and in the camps their actions were not motivated by any kind of zealous anti-Semitism, but by much more mundane factors. In his chilling description *One Day in Jozefow* Christopher Browning has detailed how one unit carried out its grim task. What emerges is that the perpetrators were influenced by peer pressure, cowardice, careerism and alcohol – all exaggerated by a brutalizing context which was entirely alien to their home environment.[3]

In all of this, one key question still dividing historians is the exact role of Hitler. Did he always intend to exterminate the Jews and did he actually give the order for the 'Final Solution'? Such questions relate back to the interpretational controversy of 'intentionalists' and

Behind Barbed Wire, by Henri Pieck, drawn in Buchenwald concentration camp.

'structuralists' mentioned in chapter 1. For historians of the intentionalist school such as Fleming or Dawidowicz,[4] Hitler remains the
key. He is seen as having committed himself to the extermination of
the Jews at an early stage in his political career, and then following a
consistent policy which led logically from the persecution of 1933 to
the gates of Auschwitz. In its simplest form they suggest that the
Holocaust happened because Hitler willed it. On the other hand, historians of the 'structuralist' school reject the idea of a long-term plan
for mass-extermination. Most notably, Schleunes has suggested that
there was no direct path because there was a lack of clear objectives and
because of the existence of rival policies. As a result the road to
Auschwitz was a 'twisted one': 'The Final Solution as it emerged in 1941
and 1942 was not the product of grand design'.[5] Instead, the 'Final
Solution', it is suggested, came to be implemented as a result of an
inner momentum within the regime – a result of the chaotic nature of
government in which various institutions and individuals improvised a
policy out of the chaotic military and human situation in eastern
Europe by the end of 1941. According to such interpretations, moral
responsibility for the 'Final Solution' extends beyond Hitler to the
apparatus of the polycratic regime (nearly all 'structuralist' historians
emphasise that this in no way reduces the guilt of Hitler himself, who
was in total agreement with such a policy). Mommsen, for example,
concluded his analysis as follows: 'It cannot be proved, for instance,
that Hitler himself gave the order for the Final Solution, though this
does not mean that he did not approve the policy. That the solution
was put into effect is by no means to be ascribed to Hitler alone, but to
the complexity of the decision-making process in the Third Reich,
which brought about a progressive and cumulative radicalisation'.[6]

This particular historical debate has proved to be a lively one and
it looks set to run for a good while yet. The controversy has generated
a very close scrutiny and analysis of all the available evidence and yet
there is no real consensus on the precise details of how and when the
'Final Solution' came to be implemented. Certainly, no written order
from Hitler for the killing of the Jews has ever been found; but that
does not prove that there never was such an order, either written or
verbal. Also it should be remembered that Hitler's authority was such
that it encouraged initiatives from below as long as they were seen to
be in line with his overall ideological vision and clearly Hitler had
often spoken in violent and barbaric terms about the Jews from an
early stage in his political career. However, it would be fallacious to
assume from the stand-point of 1945 that genocide was therefore the
intention from the start. It now seems that the initial arrangements
for the implementation of the 'Final Solution' indicate a haphazard
and makeshift approach. If this is accepted, then it might be that the
'Final Solution' should be viewed as a pragmatic response to the confusion and chaos of war in 1941–2 rather than the culmination of
long-term ideological intent.

4 Education and Youth

KEY ISSUE What did Nazi educational policy achieve?

What is the purpose of education? It is a question you might ask yourself, for it invites any number of replies. The aims of education have varied greatly over time and from one society to another. In Nazi Germany education became merely a tool for the long-term survival of the Nazi system. In a somewhat chilling statement (threat?) Hitler expressed his views in 1933:

> When an opponent declares, 'I will not come over to your side', I calmly say, 'Your child belongs to us already ... What are you? You will pass on. Your descendants, however, now stand in the new camp. In a short time they will know nothing else but this new community.'

Education in the Third Reich was therefore intended to indoctrinate its youth so completely in the principles and ethos of National Socialism that the long-term survival of the 'New Order' would never be brought into question:

> ı National Socialism is an ideology whose claim to validity is total and does not wish to be subject to the random formation of opinion. The means of implementing this claim is through education. German youth must no longer – as in the Liberal era in the cause of so-called objec-
> 5 tivity – be confronted with the choice of whether it wishes to grow up in a spirit of materialism or idealism, of racism or internationalism, of religion or godlessness, but it must be consciously shaped according to the principles which are recognised as correct and which have shown themselves to be correct: according to the principles of the ideology of
> 10 National Socialism.   *(National Socialist Teachers' League official in 1937)*

This was to be achieved not only through the traditional structure of the educational system, but also by the development of various Nazi youth movements.

The actual organisation of the state educational system was not fundamentally altered, although by a law of 1934 control was taken from the *Länder* and centralised under the Reich Ministry of Education and Science. The Ministry was then able to adapt the existing system to suit Nazi purposes by introducing a number of internal changes. Firstly, the teaching profession itself was 'reconditioned': politically unreliable individuals were removed; special courses were arranged for those teachers who remained unconvinced by the new requirements; and the influence and interference of the NSLB (*Nationalsozialistische Lehrerbund* – National Socialist Teachers' League) continued to increase. By 1937, it included 97 per cent of all teachers. Secondly, the curricula and syllabuses were adapted. A much greater emphasis was placed on physical education, so that 15 per cent of school time was given over to it, and games teachers assumed an increased status and importance in the school hierarchy. On the academic front, German, Biology and History were the focus of special attention. The study of German language and literature was intended to create 'a consciousness of being German', and to inculcate a martial and nationalistic spirit. Amongst the list of suggested reading for 14-year-old pupils was a book entitled *The Battle of Tannenberg*, which included the following extract: 'A Russian soldier tried to bar the infiltrator's way, but Otto's bayonet slid gratingly between the Russian's ribs, so that he collapsed groaning. There it lay before him, simple and distinguished, his dream's desire, the Iron Cross'. Biology became the means by which to deliver Nazi racial theory: ethnic classification, population policy and racial genetics were all integrated into the syllabus. Not surprisingly, History was also given a special place in the Nazi curriculum so that the glories of German nationalism could be emphasised. The overall effect of these changes was described in 1937 in one report from the teachers' organisation in Bavaria:

1 The extraordinary attitude displayed by large numbers of our young people to school in general and to intellectual development in the grammar schools in particular gives rise to concern for the future. Many pupils believe that they can simply drift through for eight years
5 and secure their school leaving certificate with minimal intellectual performance. The schools receive no support whatsoever from the Hitler Youth units; on the contrary, it is those pupils who are in positions of leadership there who often display unmannerly behaviour and laziness at school. School discipline has declined to an alarming
10 extent.

One final innovation was the creation of various types of elite school, which were intended to prepare the best of Germany's youth for future political leadership. The 21 *Napolas* (National Political Educational Institutions) and the ten Adolf Hitler Schools, both for boys of secondary school age, and the three *Ordensburgen*, for boys of college age, all emphasised physical training, para-military activities and political education.

However, it was the youth movements which assumed the real responsibility for the development of the vast majority of German youth. There was a long and well-established tradition of youth organisation in Germany, but in 1933 the Hitler Youth (*Hitler Jugend* – HJ) represented only 1 per cent of the total. In the next six years its structure and membership grew remarkably.

In all four groups there was a great stress on political indoctrination, but in addition the sexes were moulded for their future roles in Nazi society. Boys engaged in endless physical and military-type activities and girls were prepared for their domestic and maternal tasks.

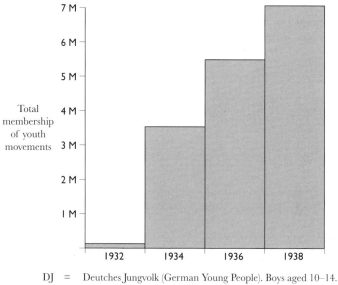

DJ = Deutches Jungvolk (German Young People). Boys aged 10–14.
HJ = Hitler Jugend (Hitler Youth). Boys aged 14–18.
JM = Jungmädelbund (League of Young Girls). Girls aged 10–14.
BDM = Bund Deutscher Mädel (League of German Girls). Girls aged 14–18.

Total membership of youth movement between 1932 and 1938.

In her memoirs, Melita Maschmann, a BDM leader, tried to put all this into perspective:

1 Apart from its beginnings during the 'years of struggle', the Hitler Youth was not a youth movement at all: it became more and more the 'state youth organisation', that is to say, it became more and more institutionalised, and finally became the instrument used by the National
5 Socialist regime to run its ideological training of young people and the war work for certain age groups.

And yet the Hitler Youth was a youth organisation. Its members may have allowed themselves to be dressed in uniforms and regimented, but they were still young people and they behaved like young people. Their
10 characteristic surplus of energy and thirst for action found great scope in their programme of activities, which constantly required great feats to be performed. It was part of the method of the National Socialist Youth leadership to arrange almost everything in the form of competitions ...
15 There was certainly a great deal of good and ambitious education in the Hitler Youth. There were groups who learned to act in a masterly way. People told stories, danced and practised handicrafts, and in these fields the regimentation was fortunately often less strict. But the idea of a competition (behind which lay the glorification of the fighter and the

20 heroic) often enough banished the element of meditation even from
musical activities, and the playful development of the creative imagin-
ation, free of any purpose, was sadly stunted.

It is notoriously difficult to assess the success of any educational
system. Above all, it depends upon the criteria used for the assessment
process, and even then, the mass of 'evidence' is open to conflicting
interpretations. Historical conclusions about Nazi education are
therefore of necessity tentative. The teaching profession certainly felt
its status to be under threat, despite its initial sympathy for the
regime. The anti-academic ethos and the facile indoctrination alienated many, whilst the Party's preference for the HJ and its activities
caused much resentment. Not surprisingly, standards in traditional
academic subjects are generally agreed to have fallen by the early
years of the war. Ironically, this was particularly the case in the various
elite schools, where physical development predominated. The impact
of the HJ seems to have been very mixed. In some respects the emphasis on team-work and extra-curricular activities was to be commended
(especially when compared to the limited provision available in other
European countries). However, the organisation suffered from its
over-rapid expansion, which made for inadequate leadership in many
areas, whilst the emphasis on military drill and discipline was certainly
resented by many adolescents.

5 Religion

> **KEY ISSUE** Did the Nazis fall short of their aim of controlling the
> Christian Churches?

Germany is the home of the Protestant Reformation. It was the Saxon
monk Martin Luther who destroyed the unity of the Catholic Church
in the sixteenth century, and the subsequent religious divisions
between Protestants and Catholics have persisted to this day. The rise
of Nazism posed profound problems for the Christian Churches. How
were they to respond to this powerful new phenomenon?

There can be little doubt that Nazism was based on a fundamentally anti-Christian philosophy. Although Hitler generally avoided
direct attacks upon the Churches in the struggle for power, and Point
24 of the Party programme spoke in favour of 'positive Christianity'
(an ambiguous phrase), it was impossible to hide the fact that the
philosophies of Nazism and Christianity were mutually antagonistic.
Christian ethics were the antithesis of Nazi values. Where Nazism
glorified strength, violence and war, Christianity taught love, forgive-
ness and neighbourly respect. Moreover, on historical grounds
Christianity was regarded as the product of an inferior race, and
therefore it could not be reconciled with Nazi *völkisch* thought. Some

leading Nazis, such as Himmler and his deputy, Heydrich, openly revealed their contempt. Hitler himself was more circumspect, although what were probably his true feelings were revealed in a private conversation in 1933:

> Neither of the denominations – Catholic or Protestant, they are both the same – has any future left ... That won't stop me stamping out Christianity in Germany root and branch. One is either a Christian or a German. You can't be both.

To what extent were such sentiments borne out in practice during the 12 years of the Third Reich? To begin with, the regime adopted a conciliatory stance towards the Churches. In his first speech as Chancellor, Hitler paid tribute to them as integral to the preservation of the nation. Members of the SA were encouraged to attend church services. This was done to give weight to the idea that Nazism coincided with nationalist Protestantism. The 'Day of Potsdam' (see page 42) further gave the impression of a unity between the Protestant Church and the state. The Catholic Church likewise succumbed to the overtures of the Nazis. Frightened by the possibility of another *Kulturkampf* (the attack on the Catholic Church made by Bismarck in the 1870s), Catholic bishops were concerned to safeguard the position of the Church under the Nazis. In 1933 a Concordat was signed between the Papacy and the regime. In return for a commitment to keep out of all political activities, the Catholic Church was guaranteed religious freedom and its pastoral and educational roles were confirmed.

However, the wooing of the Churches was totally insincere. They were merely being lulled into a false sense of security whilst the dictatorship was established. By the end of 1933 Nazi interference in religious affairs was causing resentment and disillusionment in both Catholic and Protestant Churches. The Catholic hierarchy soon discovered that the privileges promised by the Concordat were overtly disregarded: priests were harassed and arrested; Catholic schools were interfered with; and secular organisations, such as youth groups, were undermined. In the Protestant Church *Gleichschaltung* was put into effect by the so-called *Deutsche Christen* (German Christians), who managed to reconcile their evangelical piety with Nazi ideas of national renewal. A new Church constitution was formulated in 1933 with the Nazi sympathiser Ludwig Müller as first Reich Bishop – an interesting application of the *Führerprinzip*. However, such Nazi successes alienated many Protestant pastors, and there soon developed an opposition group, the *Bekennende Kirche* (Confessional Church), which upheld orthodox Lutheranism and rejected Nazi distortions. Led by Pastor Niemöller, the Confessional Church gained the support of numerous pastors, and from 1934 it claimed to represent the true Lutheran Church of Germany.

By 1935 it was clear that the Nazi *Gleichschaltung* of the Churches had achieved only limited success. Yet the Nazi leadership remained torn between a policy of suppression, which could alienate large numbers of Germans, and a policy of limited persecution, which could allow the Churches an unacceptable degree of independence outside of state control. In fact, although the ultimate objective cannot be in doubt, from 1935 Nazi tactics degenerated into a kind of war of attrition against the Churches. A Ministry of Church Affairs was established and a broad range of anti-religious measures was implemented against both Churches: the abolition of denominational schools; campaigns of vilification against the clergy; administrative restrictions; and the arrest of more and more pastors and priests (Niemöller was interned in a concentration camp in 1938). The standing of the Churches was undoubtedly weakened by this approach, but it also stimulated individual declarations of opposition, including that of the Papacy itself, which vehemently attacked the Nazi system in its encyclical, or public letter, of 1937 entitled *Mit Brennender Sorge* (*With Burning Concern*).

The outbreak of war initially brought about a more cautious policy, as the regime wished to avoid unnecessary tensions. However, following the easy military victories against Poland and France, and then the invasion of the atheistic Soviet Union, the persecution intensified. This was the result of pressure applied by anti-Christian zealots, such as Bormann and Heydrich, rather than the work of the weak and indecisive Minister of Church Affairs. Monasteries were closed, church property was attacked and church activities were severely restricted. Even so, Hitler did not allow subordination of the Churches to give way to wholesale suppression within Germany. It was only in the occupied territory of the Warthegau in Poland – the area designated as an experimental example of the 'New Order' – that events were allowed to run their logical course. Here, many of the clergy were executed, churches were closed down and the influenec of the Holy See was excluded. In the end the Nazi persecution of the Churches failed, but only because the war itself was lost.

In the place of Christianity the Nazis tried to cultivate a teutonic paganism, which became known as the German Faith Movement. Although never fully articulated, it revolved around four main themes: a wholesale rejection of Christian ethics; the propagation of the 'Blood and Soil' ideology; the exaltation of Hitler's personality; and the replacement of Christian ceremonies – marriage, baptism, etc. – by pagan equivalents. Such neo-paganism never achieved support on any large scale (the 1939 census recorded 5 per cent of the population as members of the movement), but it represented another example of how the Nazi regime tried to undermine the established Churches. The Nazis therefore achieved only limited success in their religious policy. It has been said that: 'The Churches were severely handicapped but not destroyed. Hitler's programme needed time: he was himself destroyed before it had taken root.'[7] However, as will be discussed in chapter 8, it could also be said that the Christian

Churches failed as well, in that their concern to uphold the institutions of Christianity was an abnegation of their moral duty actively to resist a reprehensible regime.

6 Women and the Family

> **KEY ISSUE** To what extent were the Nazis able to reverse the prevailing demographic and social trends?

The first quarter of the twentieth century had witnessed profound sociological changes in German family life. Germany's demographic growth had decelerated markedly (which is not to say that the actual population had declined). In 1900 there had been over 2 million live births per annum, whereas by 1933 the figure was below 1 million. Over the same period female employment expanded by at least a third, far outstripping the percentage increase in population. Both of these trends had been partially brought about by long-term changes in social behaviour common to many industrialised countries. In particular, there was the recognition by many people that an improved standard of living would result from the use of contraception to limit family size, and the desire of a better educated female population to have a vocation as well as children. However, Germany's particular historical circumstances also exaggerated these developments. Economic mobilisation during the war had driven women into the factories, whilst post-war the difficulties caused by inflation had encouraged them to stay there out of economic necessity. In addition, the war had left a surplus of 1.8 million marriageable women, as well as many wives with invalided husbands. Finally, economic reorientation in the 1920s had led to an increased demand for non-manual labour and the growth of mass-production techniques requiring more unskilled workers, both of which tended to favour the employment of women, who could be paid less than men.

The ideology of National Socialism was in stark contrast to these developments. It fundamentally opposed the social and economic emancipation of women. Indeed, Nazi anti-feminism has been viewed as a kind of secondary racism in which women in the Third Reich were the victims of a sexist-racist male regime which reduced women to the status of mere objects.[8] Such an interpretation would have been denied by the Nazis, who claimed to regard women as different rather than inferior. In their view, nature had ordained that the two sexes should fulfil entirely different roles, and it was simply the task of the Nazi state to maintain this distinction. What this amounted to in practice was that 'a woman's place was to be in the home'. Or, as the Nazi slogan presented it, they were to be devoted to the three Ks – *'Kinder, Küche, Kirche'* ('children, kitchen and church'). Such dogma was upheld by the Party even before 1933 – there was not a single female Nazi deputy in the Reichstag, and a Party regulation of 1921 excluded women from all senior positions within its structure.

Nazi views on women tied in with their concern about the demographic trends. A growing population was viewed as a sign of national strength and martial vigour – a reflection of Germany's aspiration to superpower status. How could they demand *Lebensraum* in eastern Europe, if the number of Germans was in fact levelling out? It was therefore considered essential to bring about a substantial increase in the population and to this end women were portrayed as primarily the mothers of the next generation – an image which suited Nazi anti-feminism. However, Nazi policy objectives for women and the family in no way reflected the social realities of twentieth-century Germany.

Initially, attempts to reduce the number of women in work seem to have been quite successful. Between 1933 and 1936 married women were in turn debarred from jobs in medicine, law and the higher ranks of the civil service. Moreover, the number of female teachers and university students was reduced considerably. Such legislation had a profound effect on professional middle-class women, although their actual number was small. In other sectors of the economy a mixture of Party pressure and financial inducements was employed to cajole women out of the work-place and back into the home. From June 1933 interest-free loans of 600RM were made available to young women who withdrew from the labour market in order to get married. The effects of the Depression also worked in the favour of Nazi objectives, since it not only drastically reduced the number of female workers (although proportionately far less than male workers), but it also enabled the government to justify its campaign for women to give up work for the benefit of unemployed men. On these grounds, labour exchanges and employers were advised to discriminate positively in favour of men. As a result of all this, although employment of women between 1932 and 1937 rose from 4.8 million to 5.9 million, it fell from 37 per cent to 31 per cent of the total.

Women were quite specifically excluded from the job market. The only opportunity available in this sphere was within the various Nazi women's organisations, such as the NSF (*National Sozialistische Frauenschaft* – National Socialist Womanhood) and the DFW (*Deutsches Frauenwerk* – German Women's Enterprise). Yet, the NSF and DFW were regarded by the Party as mere tools for the propagation of the anti-feminist ideology by means of cultural, educational and social programmes. And so, when a campaign started in the NSF for enhanced opportunities for women within the Party, its organisers were officially discredited.

However, by 1937 Nazi ideological convictions were already threatened by the pressures of economic necessity. The introduction of conscription and the rearmament declaration in 1935 soon led to an increasing shortage of labour as the Nazi economy continued to grow.

The anti-feminist ideology could only be upheld if economic growth was slowed down and that, in turn, would curtail the rearmament programme. This, of course, Hitler was not prepared to sanction. Consequently, market forces inevitably began to exploit this readily available pool of labour, and the relative decline in female employment was reversed. Between 1937 and 1939 it rose from 5.9 million to 6.9 million, and from 31 per cent to 33 per cent of the total. In this situation the government even decided to end the arrangement whereby women who withdrew from the labour market would qualify for the marriage loan scheme.

The contradictions between theory and practice were exacerbated further with the onset of war. Germany's economic mobilisation was at first badly organised and not very efficient (see pages 60–1). So, although there was no general conscription of female labour, the number of women at work continued to increase. In such a situation working women experienced considerable hardship. Long hours in an arms factory or the continuous demands of running a farm made life very arduous, especially if there were the added responsibilities of maintaining a household and raising children. Thus, when from 1943 Speer did try to mobilise the economy on a total war footing by suggesting the conscription of women workers, he encountered opposition from Bormann, Sauckel (the Plenipotentiary for Labour) and indeed from Hitler himself, who was always concerned about civilian morale. The Nazis were caught in the contradictions of their own ideology. In the final two years of the Nazi state more and more women ended up at work, and yet the government could not bring itself to renounce fully its anti-feminist rhetoric. An official in the NSF wrote, 'It has always been our chief article of faith that a woman's place is in the home – but since the whole of Germany is our home we must serve wherever we can best do so'.[9]

Of course, the dilemma facing the Nazi state was made worse by its obsessive desire to increase Germany's population. This was encouraged in a number of ways: the enforcement of anti-abortion laws; the restriction of contraceptive advice and facilities; improved maternity benefits and family allowances; and the conversion of one-quarter of the marriage loan scheme into a straight gift from the state for each child born. Inevitably, this was all backed up by an extensive propaganda campaign, which glorified motherhood and the large family. There were also rewards: the Honour Cross of the German Mother in bronze, silver and gold, awarded for four, six and eight children respectively. Such glorification reached its sickening climax in the coining of the Nazi slogan 'I have donated a child to the Führer' (as contemporary humorists soon pointed out, this was presumably because of Hitler's personal unwillingness or inability to father children of his own).

Statistics do show quite clearly that from a low-point in 1933 the birth-rate did increase, reaching a peak in 1939, although thereafter it again slowly declined. The problem for the historian is deciding whether Nazi population policy was actually responsible for this demographic trend. Interpreting population statistics is notoriously difficult because it involves so many different factors – sociological, economic, and even personal psychological factors. Thus, any mono-causal explanation is almost certain to be incorrect. Yet, trying to assess the *relative* significance of Nazi population policy against the importance of the end of the Depression, or the general trend to marry younger is fraught with problems. In this case, the cautious analysis, which merely accepts the interaction of these various causes, is more likely to be closer to historical reality.

One other significant factor of Nazi population policy was its aim not only to bring about a quantitative increase but also a qualitative improvement. Eugenic policy aimed to limit by sterilisation the repro-duction of those people with hereditary diseases or anti-social behav-ioural problems such as alcoholism, and by 1939 375,000 such people had been forcibly sterilised. It also led to the establishment of one of the weirdest features of Nazi social engineering, *Lebensborn* (Spring of Life) – an institution which nominally cared for unmarried mothers of good racial credentials, but which also made the necessary arrange-ments for girls to be 'impregnated' by members of the SS.

Nazi views on women and the family were a natural concomitant to their rhetoric about the *Mittelstand*. As such, their ideological inten-tions were irreconcilable with the realities of twentieth-century Germany, and indeed clearly clashed with the Nazi objectives of rear-mament and military conquest. Consequently, Nazi policy towards women and the family was contradictory and incoherent, and did little to affect the ongoing sociological trends of an industrialised society.

7 Cultural Life

KEY ISSUE Did the Third Reich manage to create a cultural identity of its own?

During the evening of 10 May 1933 in the middle of a square just off *Unter den Linden* in Berlin there took place an event which soon became known as 'the burning of the books'. Thousands of tomes seized from private and public libraries were hurled into the flames by Nazi activists because they were considered undesirable on account of their Jewish, socialist or pacifist tendencies. For a nation whose lit-erary heritage was perhaps greater than any other nation's in Europe, it was seen by many Germans and non-Germans alike as an act of mindless barbarism. It also rather aptly set the tone for the cultural life of Nazi Germany.

Culture was no longer to be encouraged according to the axiom of 'art for art's sake'. Rather, it was to serve the purpose of moulding public opinion, and with this in mind the Reich Chamber of Culture was supervised by the Propaganda Ministry. Germany's cultural life during the Third Reich was simply to be yet another means of achieving censorship and indoctrination, although Dr Goebbels expressed it in more high-falutin language:

> What we are aiming for is more than a revolt. Our historic mission is to transform the very spirit itself to the extent that people and things are brought into a new relationship with one another.

Culture was therefore 'co-ordinated' by means of the Reich Chamber of Culture, established in 1933, which made provision for seven sub-chambers: fine arts, music, the theatre, the press, radio, literature and films. In this way, just as anyone in the media had no option but to toe the Party line (see page 104), so all those involved in cultural activities had to be accountable for their creativity.

What kind of image did Goebbels hope to project and how was this achieved? Nazi culture was permeated by a number of key themes reflecting the usual ideological prejudices: anti-Semitism; militarism and the glorification of war; nationalism and the supremacy of the Aryan race; the cult of the Führer and the power of absolutism; anti-modernism and the theme of 'Blood and Soil'; neo-paganism and a repudiation of traditional Christian values.

The world of music managed to cope reasonably well in this environment, partly because of its less obvious political overtones and partly because of Germany's rich classical tradition, which was proudly exploited by the regime. However, Mahler and Mendelssohn, both great Jewish composers, were banned, as were most modern developments. The new wave of classical composers, Stravinsky, Schoenberg and Hindemith, were disparaged and the new 'genres' of jazz and dance-band were respectively labelled 'negroid' and 'decadent'.

Over 2,500 of Germany's literary community left their homeland during the years 1933–45. This fact alone is a sad reflection upon how such German writers and dramatists as Thomas Mann and Bertolt Brecht viewed the new cultural atmosphere. Their place was taken by a 'second XI', who either sympathised with the regime or accepted the curbs. It is difficult to identify a single book, play or poem written during the Third Reich, and officially blessed by the regime, which has stood the test of time.

Actors, like the musicians, tended to content themselves with productions of the classics – Schiller, Goethe (and Shakespeare) – in the knowledge that such plays were politically acceptable and in the best traditions of German theatre. The visual arts were also effectively regimented by the Nazi constraints. Modern schools were held in total contempt and Weimar's rich cultural awakening was rejected as degenerate and symbolic of the moral and political decline of

Comrades by Arno Breker. Breker was sculptor-in-chief to the Third Reich. By collaborating closely with Albert Speer he undertook numerous government commissions.

Germany under a system of parliamentary democracy. Instead, encouragement was given to works depicting the traditional Nazi themes in a mould of classical realism. As one historian has said: 'The best that can be said of the kind of painting and sculpture that was honoured by the Nazi movement was that it was no worse than the socialist realism in the Soviet Union'.[10]

Only in the field of film can it be said that the Nazi regime made a genuine cultural contribution. Germany's cinematic reputation had been established in the 1920s, but continuity was maintained as many of the major film studios were in the hands of nationalist sympathisers. Goebbels recognised the importance of this expanding form of entertainment and, on the whole, managed to reconcile political objectives with the integrity of the film-makers (only 96 out of 1,097 feature films produced between 1933 and 1945 were specifically at the request of the Propaganda Ministry). As a result, the talents of many 'Nazi' directors, such as Leni Riefenstahl, are still held in high regard by film buffs for their use of cinematic techniques to evoke great emotions despite the underlying political messages.

In the play *Schlageter* (1934) by Hanns Johst there is the line, 'Whenever I hear the word culture, I reach for my gun'. It is a phrase which is often, and wrongly, attributed to Göring, but its acceptance by the Nazi authorities neatly underlines their philistine approach. Cultural life during the Third Reich was effectively muzzled – it could

---

A.

There was once a nanny-goat who said,
In my cradle someone sang to me:
'A strong man is coming.
He will set you free!'

The ox looked at her askance.
Then turning to the pig
He said,
'That will be the butcher'. (Bertolt Brecht)

B.

W. Beumelburg, *Gruppe Bosemüller*. In a trench in World War One Corporal Wammsch offers to send Private Siewers on leave following the latter's loss of nerve.

'But I don't want to go away ... I have to make up for something ... give me time, why won't you give me some time? I don't want to go home, I don't want my leave ... I don't want it ... I want to go back to Fleury and the Souville ravine ... that's all I want.'

He is sobbing and shaking as if in a fever.

Wammsch is terribly afraid. He hadn't expected this.

'I don't want to go home ... I'll go down on my knees before the captain ... he will listen to me ... I don't want to go home to my mother ... I want to go to the Souville ravine and Fleury again.'

Now he is exhausted at last. He is still sobbing and his whole body heaves. But he no longer resists. He calmly lets himself be taken into Wammsch's embrace, lets himself be carressed by Wammsch's hard hands, and there is something wonderfully dissolving in this feeling.

'There ...' says Wammsch, deeply moved, 'I'll go straight to the captain and talk to him. Of course you'll stay with us. The first one to give you an old-fashioned look is going to get my fist in his face ...'

only operate within the Nazi strait-jacket and to that extent Goebbels succeeded. However, the regime most certainly failed in its attempts to create a Nazi cultural identity firmly rooted in the minds of the *Volk*. Some might suggest that it was simply a question of time, and that the regime's success in building new theatres and libraries and attracting more people to cultural events would have eventually brought about the desired result. On the other hand, the very powerful cultural resurgence throughout Germany since 1945 suggests that the traditions and spirit of Germany's cultural identity were too deeply imbued to be expunged by an essentially destructive and negative force such as Nazism.

8 A Social Revolution?

> **KEY ISSUES** In what ways has Nazism been seen as socially revolutionary? How tenable is the view that the Third Reich had a revolutionary impact?

At first sight it might seem strange even to suggest that Germany underwent a 'social revolution' during the Third Reich, for Nazism was a movement of the extreme right, and revolutions are normally associated with left-wing political parties. However, as academic interest in the social consequences of Nazism has grown since the 1960s, two major theses have developed which have supported the notion of Nazism's revolutionary impact on German society.

In his book *Hitler's Social Revolution*, published in 1966, David Schoenbaum argued that Nazism was a powerful modernising force in German society. His interpretation is a complex one founded on the differentiation between what he describes as 'objective' and 'interpreted' social reality. Thus, on the face of it, he accepted that the Third Reich witnessed many of the typical changes one associates with a developing industrial society ('objective social reality'). However, many of these changes were at odds with the backward-looking ideology of Nazism. This glaring contradiction was countered, he claims, by the Nazis successfully projecting an image of a society devoid of the traditional ties of class and status. Thus, Nazi society was regarded by the people as 'united like no other in recent German history, a society of opportunities for young and old, classes and masses, a society that was New Deal and good old days at the same time'. In effect, the idea of the *Volksgemeinschaft*, of a community of Germans working together regardless of background or role in society, was the reality of the Third Reich as perceived in the minds of its citizens ('interpreted social reality'). In this sense, at least, Schoenbaum suggests the Third Reich witnessed a fundamental change in social values and attitudes, which formed the basis of a revolutionary national consensus.[11]

Painting by Diego Rivera, 1933. Rivera (1886–1957) was a Mexican painter though he spent a lot of time in the 1920s and 1930s in Europe and the USA. He was a leading figure of early twentieth-century revolutionary art. His folk-art style reflects his strong sympathy for the peasant and proletariat.

Another interpretation which has gained increasing currency of late is the idea of 'a revolution of destruction'. According to this view, the changes in Nazi society, whether objective or interpreted, were so limited, incoherent and lacking in permanence that the idea of social revolution is without substance. Instead, the real revolution is seen to be in the destruction wrought by the effects of total war – wholesale military defeat and occupation, the break-up of a united Germany and its eventual political division, massive economic dislocation, and the demise of the social elites and vested interests which had dominated German life since the mid-nineteenth century.

Such interpretations have found little favour with those historians who point to the realities of the prevailing class structure in the Third Reich. For Marxists schooled in the tradition of East German historiography, any idea of social revolution in Germany before the arrival of the liberating ideology of Soviet Communism and the creation of the Communist People's Republic (1949) is nonsense. In their view, Nazism was not social revolution but social reaction of the worst kind since it reinforced traditional class alignments and strengthened the position of the establishment elites, especially the powerful interests of the military and capitalism, at the expense of more popular institutions, such as trade unions.

Of all the disputes about the Third Reich, the 'social revolution' versus 'social reaction' is one of the most complex. The mere definition of terms such as 'reaction' and 'revolution' is very difficult, and often becomes the focus of argument in its own right. Likewise, Nazism itself defies straightforward analysis. It was a unique mixture of forces which reflected a broad and varied social make-up. Therefore, when one tears away the propaganda and asks 'what were the real social aims of the Third Reich?' and 'did the Third Reich achieve those aims?', unfortunately the answers remain very murky. It is difficult to gauge the direct impact of Nazism – as opposed to the effects of other forces for change. Germany's history in the first half of the twentieth century is tumultuous and German society had been experiencing great changes in the 60 years before 1933. The Nazis were in power for only twelve years and six of those were spent fighting the bloodiest war in human history. Can the historian draw a line between Nazism and the war as a catalyst for social change? Should he try to draw that line, when it could be argued that war was a natural feature of Nazism? These are the kinds of questions which make any analysis of the Third Reich's social impact an extraordinarily complex task.

In spite of such problems of interpretation, it is difficult to see the Nazi movement in power as exerting a revolutionary impact. Elements of the Party which did support radical social change were silenced; the framework of the existing class structure was not altered; and the concept of the *Volksgemeinschaft* was little more than an effective propaganda ploy. Schoenbaum's thesis is not easily disproved, but equally his view of a revolutionary change in popular attitudes and outlook is difficult to substantiate. However, past experience generally suggests that attempts to bring about fundamental changes in attitude are notoriously difficult to effect. In reality, Nazism could not reconcile its own rather confused social ideology with the ongoing pressures for change within a developing industrial society. These contradictions were further exaggerated by the requirements of political pragmatism once the Third Reich was set on its course of territorial expansion and ultimately war. Thus, despite Nazi rhetorical support for the *Mittelstand* and the peasantry, both groups came under enormous social and economic pressure, and instead it was the traditional elites which continued to dominate and prosper. Women were supposed to stay at home and have more children, but their role tended to suit the economic demands of the situation. The Christian Churches were expected to wither away, but they survived. Nazi culture was meant to establish new roots in the *Volk*, but it exerted little more than a negative censorious role. If there was a revolutionary core to Nazism, one might argue that it is to be found in the obsessive nature and implementation of its racial policy. Otherwise, it is difficult to escape the conclusion that there was no accelerated social transformation in Germany between 1933 and 1945.

However, such an interpretation is not incompatible with the view that a revolution in German society took place in the *wake* of the Third Reich. A simple comparison and contrast between the years 1933, 1945 and 1957 makes the point. The social changes in Germany between 1945 and 1957 were far more substantial than in the previous twelve years. Certainly, continuities prevailed – cultural traditions and social institutions, such as the family and the Churches, do not break down overnight. However, the wholesale collapse of the Third Reich also brought to an end Prussian militarism and its social basis, the *Junker* landed aristocracy. It also led to the political division of Germany and the creation of two states with very different social and economic conditions, both of which were the result of alien cultures and political philosophies in the form of Anglo-American and Soviet occupying forces. Perhaps, ironically, this was the real revolutionary legacy of Nazism.

References

1 J. Noakes & G. Pridham, *Nazism 1919–45*, Vol 1, (Exeter, 1983) p. 4
2 D. Goldhagen, *Hitler's Willing Executioners: Ordinary Germans and the Holocaust* (London, 1996)
3 C. Browning, *Ordinary Men* (New York, 1992)
4 L. Dawidowicz, *The War against the Jews* (Weidenfeld & Nicholson, 1975)
   G. Fleming, *Hitler and the Final Solution* (London, 1986)
5 K. Schleunes, *The Twisted Road to Auschwitz* (London, 1970) p. 2
6 H. Mommsen, 'The Realization of the Unthinkable. The Final Solution of the Jewish Question in the Third Reich' in H. Mommsen, *From Weimar to Auschwitz* (Oxford, 1991) pp. 224–53

7   J.R.C. Wright, *Above Parties* (Oxford, 1974) p. 195
8   See G. Bock, 'Anti-natalism, Maternity and Paternity in National Socialist Racism' in D. Crew (ed.) *Nazism and German Society* (Routledge, 1994)
9   R. Grünberger, *A Social History of the Third Reich* (Penguin, 1974) p. 328
10 G. Craig, *Germany 1866–1945* (OUP, 1981) p. 653
11 D. Schoenbaum, *Hitler's Social Revolution* (London, 1966)

Summary Diagram
The social and racial impact of the Third Reich

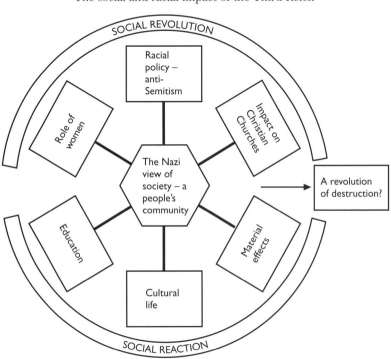

Working on Chapter 5

This is a difficult chapter to study in a number of respects: some of the ideas and terminology – both those put forward by the Nazis and those used by historians – are difficult to understand; and there is also a fair amount of detail. To start with it would be useful if your notes contained your own definition/explanation of the word *Volksgemeinschaft*. In each of sections 2–7 you need to go into a fair amount of detail. However, it is important that you do not become so swamped with facts that you lose sight of the broader issues. With each section it would be a good idea to keep the following questions in mind *throughout*:

i) What were the theoretical aims of Nazism in this particular field?
ii) To what extent was the theory reflected in reality?
iii) In what ways were Nazi theory and practice compatible and incompatible with each other?

Having written your notes for each section it would also be useful in each case to write summary answers to the questions in the issues boxes.

Section 8 is by far the most difficult. But make certain you at least write down a brief explanation of how and why Nazi social policy might be defined as: a) 'a revolution of destruction', b) 'unreservedly reactionary', and, c) 'a revolution based on interpreted social reality'. You will probably want to come back to this section when you have read chapter 8 and understood a little more of the debate regarding popular attitudes.

Answering structured and essay questions on Chapter 5

In this chapter you have looked at the social impact of the Third Reich in its broadest sense and hopefully you have begun to grapple with many of the issues raised. In preparing to answer structured and essay questions on this topic it is vitally important that you are aware of the exact extent of your knowledge and the particular demands of each question. Some questions will focus on a very specific area of content, others will be much broader in their coverage. You must therefore be clear in your own mind that you have the necessary depth or breadth in terms of factual knowledge and analytical skills to answer a particular question.

It is quite possible that in one part of a structured question you will be asked to give a straightforward description. This would then be followed up by more demanding questions in which you will be required to explain and analyse developments or assess interpretations. But at least you are being directed in the structured questions. Look at the following examples:

1. a) Outline briefly Nazi anti-Semitic policy in the years 1933–5.
   b) In what ways did *Kristallnacht* mark a turning-point in the Nazi treatment of the Jews?
   c) Why have historians found it difficult to agree on the motives for implementing the 'Final Solution'?
2. a) Explain briefly the attitudes of the Christian Churches to the establishment of the Nazi regime in 1933.
   b) Why were the Churches never 'co-ordinated' like other major institutions in Germany?
   c) Would you agree that the Churches failed to offer adequate resistance to the Nazi regime?

Whereas structured questions usually direct you towards the relevant areas, essay questions require you to decide what is relevant and expect you to shape the material accordingly. Clearly this is more demanding and it is vital that you unlock essay questions appropriately before you start writing. Study the following questions:

1. Why was Hitler able to make his own personal anti-Semitism such a powerful feature of German society?
2. Would you agree that the aim of creating a *Volksgemeinschaft* led to revolutionary changes in German society?
3. Examine and explain the changing relationship between the Christian Churches and the Nazi regime.
4. Did Nazi social and economic policies bring any benefit to the German people up to the outbreak of war?
5. 'While man makes his supreme sacrifice on the field of battle woman fights her supreme battle for her nation when she gives life to her child.' To what extent was the Nazi view of women actually put into practice?
6. Examine the impact of the Third Reich on German cultural life.

With each of these essay questions, ask yourself what exactly is required for a good answer:

a) Does it focus on one, several or all the aspects of Third Reich social history?
b) Does it need a knowledge of material from other topics in the history of the Third Reich?
c) What exactly are the chronological parameters of the question?
d) What kind of question is it: causation, comparison or assessment?

Of course it is not enough just to cover the correct factual material. You must also satisfy the analytical demands of the question. At first sight question 6 might appear the easiest and question 2 the hardest. But to gain high marks on question 6 you would have to go beyond a mere description of Nazi cultural policy. You would need to discuss at least the following four sub-questions:

a) What is meant by the word 'culture'?
b) What did Nazi culture stand for?
c) Was Nazi culture merely an extension of the propaganda machine?
d) How does the period of the Third Reich compare with earlier and later periods of German cultural history?

Looking for sub-questions within essay questions is a very good way of unlocking them.

On the other hand, although question 2 appears daunting, you should be able to tackle it, if you have digested the contents of this chapter well. Draw up a list of 5 sub-questions which will allow you to unlock question 2; re-order them with the intention of each sub-question forming the basis of a paragraph of the essay; and finally, write out a conclusion in full, making certain you get back to the fundamental issue of the original question.

Source-based questions on Chapter 5

1. Anti-Semitism

Read the extracts from Maschmann, Himmler and Höss on pages 71 and 72. Study the painting by Pieck on page 73. Answer the following questions.

a) In what ways do Maschmann's memoirs help to explain the development of anti-Semitism in Nazi Germany? (*4 marks*)

b) Pieck's picture was painted in Buchenwald concentration camp in 1943. What was the artist trying to communicate? Explain your answer in detail. (*5 marks*)

c) Compare and contrast the statements of Höss and Himmler. (*4 marks*)

d) The Holocaust poses profound problems of interpretation for the historian. What are the problems of evaluation highlighted by these four sources? (*6 marks*)

e) To what extent do these sources and other evidence known to you support the view that the Holocaust was the inevitable result of Nazi anti-Semitic policy? (*7 marks*)

2. Culture

Read the two written extracts by Brecht and Beumelburg on page 87. Study the two pieces of art on pages 86 and 89. Answer the following questions:

a) Which of the two written extracts was banned by the Nazi regime? Explain your answer fully by reference to both passages. (*6 marks*)

b) What was Breker trying to communicate in his sculpture? (*4 marks*)

c) Explain fully why you think that Rivera's painting was not allowed to be exhibited in Germany until after 1945. (*4 marks*)

d) 'The historian can learn more about a society by studying what it has censored rather than what it has officially endorsed.' Do you agree? Explain your answer fully with reference to the above sources and to your overall understanding of Nazi Germany. (*6 marks*)

3. Education

Read the extracts on pages 75, 76 and 77. Answer the following questions:

a) According to the extract from the official of the National Socialist Teachers' League, what were the main aims of education in the Third Reich? (*3 marks*)

b) What major problems in German education are highlighted in the report? How useful is such a report in assessing the effectiveness of Nazi educational policy? (*6 marks*)

c) Do you think that Maschmann provides an objective view of the Hitler Youth? Explain your answer. (*4 marks*)

d) 'Nazi indoctrination of German youth was one of the more successful elements of its social programme.' Do you agree? (*7 marks*)

6 The Political Structure of the Third Reich

POINTS TO CONSIDER

There are many common misapprehensions and over-simplifications about the political structure of the Third Reich. Your initial reading should begin to give you a more informed insight into the more complex realities. As you do this, it is important for you to:
a) recognise the range of competing political and economic forces
b) appreciate the key turning-points in the relationship between these forces
c) assess the validity of 'totalitarianism' as a term to describe the Third Reich.

KEY DATES

1934	June	Night of the Long Knives.
1936	June	Appointment of Heinrich Himmler as chief of the German Police.
	Oct	Introduction of the Four Year Plan under the control of Göring; followed in the next year by the resignation of Schacht. Big business weakened.
1938	Feb	Forced resignation of Field Marshal Blomberg (Minister of Defence) and General Fritsch (Army Commander-in-Chief); mini-purge of Army.
1939	Sept	Creation of RSHA.
1942–3	Winter	Military 'turn of the tide'; German defeats at El Alamein and at Stalingrad.
1944	July	Stauffenberg Bomb Plot; Army purged.

1 The Concept of Totalitarianism

> **KEY ISSUES** What is meant by 'totalitarianism'? Why has the term been applied to the Third Reich?

In his futuristic novel *Nineteen Eighty-Four* George Orwell portrayed a political system and a society which has subsequently become a 'model' of totalitarianism. There was no place for the individual in *Nineteen Eighty-Four*, every aspect of life was controlled by the party, which in turn was dominated by the all-pervasive personality of 'Big Brother'. Such was the extent of this totalitarian control that tele-screens in every room observed one's actions, whilst the thought police tracked down anyone whose beliefs were incompatible with party ideology. In such fictional ways Orwell took the concept of totalitarianism to its logical and absurd conclusion.

Orwell was writing in the late 1940s and his vision of totalitarianism had been stimulated to a large extent by his observations of the dictatorial regimes of the period, especially Stalin's (which is a very good reason why you, as a student of twentieth-century history, should try to read Orwell's book). However, in the 1950s a number of historians and political scientists also began to interpret the Nazi regime as an example of the totalitarian model. According to such interpretations there were no fundamental differences between the regimes of Fascist Italy, Nazi Germany and Soviet Russia. Indeed, Carl Friedrich's analysis went so far as to identify six major features common to totalitarian dictatorships: an official ideology, a single mass party, terroristic control by the police, monopolistic control over the media, a monopoly of arms, and central control of the economy – all of which he claimed existed in Mussolini's Italy, Hitler's Germany and Stalin's Russia.[1]

Although the idea of Nazism as a form of totalitarianism held great sway in the 1950s, such a view is not now so readily accepted. However, you will often still see the term used to describe Hitler's regime. This chapter therefore examines the *balance* of forces and interest groups in the political and economic life of the Third Reich. You should bear in mind the concept of totalitarianism and assess whether the power structure which emerges can be equated with it.

2 The Nazi System of Government

> **KEY ISSUE** How powerful were the various party organs in the Nazi system of government?

a) The Relationship between Party and State

By July 1933 Germany had become a one-party state, in which the Nazi Party claimed sole political authority in every aspect of German life. Such totalitarian claims, augmented by a powerful propaganda machine, deceived many contemporaries into thinking that the Nazi state was a clear and well-ordered system of government. The reality was very different. Fundamentally, this was because the exact relationship between the structure and role of the Party on the one hand and the apparatus of the German state on the other was never to be clarified satisfactorily.

From the start, the existence of parallel Party and state machinery laid the basis for much of the confusion. Some of the Nazi leaders were keen to establish the Party's control over the civil and diplomatic services. This to some extent reflected the wishes of the revolutionary elements within the Party, which wanted to smash such traditional elements of government in order to create a new kind of Germany –

although it also conveniently provided an avenue for self-advancement. However, others recognised that the bureaucracy of the German state was well established and staffed by an educated personnel, which could not simply be disregarded. Initially, therefore, there was no drastic purge of the state apparatus. The *Law for the Restoration of the Professional Civil Service* of April 1933 was strictly limited in its scope. It only provided for the removal of Jews and known opponents of the regime.

Hitler himself also remained ambivalent on the issue, despite attempts from both sides to seek clarification. The *Law to ensure the Unity of Party and State* promulgated in December 1933 proclaimed that the Party 'is inseparably linked with the state', but the explanation was phrased in such nebulous terms as to be meaningless. Two months later, Hitler declared that the Party's principal responsibilities were to implement government measures and to organise propaganda and indoctrination. Yet, in September 1934 he told the Party Congress that 'it is not the state which commands us but rather we who command the state', and a year later he specifically declared that the Party would assume responsibility for those tasks which the state failed to fulfil.

Hitler's ambiguity on this issue is partially explained by the political ferment of these years and by the need to placate numerous interest groups. However, the problem was also rooted in the background and composition of the Party itself. The Party organisation had been created and had evolved as a means to *gain* political power. It had proved remarkably well designed for this purpose, but it was not geared to the task of government. Moreover, the Party itself was by no means a unified whole. It consisted of a mass of specialist organisations – such as the Hitler Youth, the German Labour Front and the NS Teachers' League. Such groups had evolved because of the need to attract support from different sections of society in the years before 1933. Once in power, such groups were keen to uphold their own particular interests – the Party had become splintered and lacked a unifying structure.

Another problem emerged in the course of 1933. As the Nazi regime established itself a vast increase in Party membership took place as people jumped on the bandwagon of opportunity. This tended to dilute the influence of the old guard, thus further weakening the radical cutting edge of the Party apparatus within the regime.

However, the position of the Party did improve somewhat from the mid-1930s when Rudolf Hess, as Deputy Führer, was granted special powers. In 1935 he was given the right to vet the appointment and promotion of all civil servants, and to oversee the drafting of all legislation. By 1939 it had become compulsory for all civil servants to be Party members. In this way, the foundations were laid for Party supervision, if not outright domination, of the state apparatus.

The other key figure in the changing fortunes of the Party was Martin Bormann, who was a skilled and hard-working administrator with great personal ambition. Working alongside Hess, he correctly analysed the problems confronting the Party and created two new departments with the deliberate aim of strengthening the Party's position (and thereby his own). These were the Department for Internal Party Affairs, which had the task of exerting discipline within the Party structure, and the Department for Affairs of State, which aimed to secure Party supremacy over the state. Considerable success was achieved by these two departments in subsequent years, especially after 1941 when Hess's flight to England further strengthened Bormann's personal position. Thereafter, by constant meddling, by sheer perseverance and by maintaining good personal relations with Hitler, Bormann effectively advanced the Party's fortunes. By 1943, when he officially became Hitler's Secretary, and thus secured direct access to the Führer, Bormann had constructed an immensely strong power-base for himself.

Under Bormann's influence the Party was moulded into an institution of government rather than merely of opposition. It also succeeded in strengthening its position in respect of the traditional apparatus of the state. Undoubtedly, therefore, it was one of the key power blocs within Nazi Germany, and its influence continued to be felt until the very end. However, it must be remembered that the Party had to compete strenuously for influence with the state institutions, and the latter were never emasculated, even if they were circumscribed. Above all, the internal divisions and rivalries within the Party itself were never entirely overcome and consequently the Nazi Party never became such an all-pervasive dominating instrument as the Communist Party did in Soviet Russia.

b) The Role of Hitler

What exactly was the role of Hitler himself in the political labyrinth of the Third Reich? In theory his power was unlimited. Nazi Germany was a one-party state and Hitler was undisputed leader of that Party. In addition, after the death of Hindenburg in August 1934, the *Law concerning the Head of State of the German Reich* combined the posts of President and Chancellor. Constitutionally, Hitler was also Commander-in-Chief of all the armed services.

However, if one studies contemporary documents, such as this extract from a leading Nazi theorist, it is clear that Hitler's personal dictatorship was portrayed in more than purely legal terms:

1 The office of Führer has developed out of the National Socialist movement. In its origins it is not a state office. The office of Führer has grown out of the movement into the Reich ... The position of Führer combines in itself all sovereign power of the Reich: all public power in
5 the state as in the movement is derived from the Führer's power. If we wish to define political power in the *völkisch Reich* correctly, we must

not speak of 'state power' but of 'Führer power'. For it is not the state
as an impersonal entity which is the source of political power, but
rather political power is given to the Führer as the executor of the
10 nation's common will. 'Führer power' is comprehensive and total: it
unites within itself all means of creative political activity: it embraces all
spheres of national life.[2]

Such grandiose theoretical claims for 'Führer power' could not mask
basic practical problems. Firstly, there was (and is) no way one individual could ever be in control of all aspects of government. Thus
Hitler was still dependent upon sympathetic subordinates to put
policy decisions into effect (just as the mere passage of an Act of
Parliament in Britain will never guarantee to solve a problem unless
the apparatus for effective implementation exists). Additionally,
Hitler's own personality and attitude towards administration were not
conducive to strong and effective leadership of government. At first
this may seem rather contrary to the idea of Hitler as the charismatic
and dynamic leader. However, this was an image perpetuated by the
propaganda machine and once in government Hitler's true character
revealed itself, as is shown in the memoirs of one of his retinue:

1 Hitler normally appeared shortly before lunch ... When Hitler stayed
at Obersalzberg it was even worse. There he never left his room before
2.00 pm. He spent most afternoons taking a walk, in the evening straight
after dinner, there were films ... He disliked the study of documents. I
5 have sometimes secured decisions from him without his ever asking to
see the relevant files. He took the view that many things sorted themselves out on their own if one did not interfere ... He let people tell
him the things he wanted to hear, everything else he rejected. One still
sometimes hears the view that Hitler would have done the right thing
10 if people surrounding him had not kept him wrongly informed. Hitler
refused to let himself be informed ... How can one tell someone the
truth who immediately gets angry when the facts do not suit him.[3]

A slightly different view was presented by Hitler's press chief:

1 In the twelve years of his rule in Germany Hitler produced the biggest
confusion in government that has ever existed in a civilised state.
During his period of government, he removed from the organisation of
the state all clarity of leadership. It was not all laziness or an excessive
5 degree of tolerance which led the otherwise so energetic and forceful
Hitler to tolerate this real witch's cauldron of struggles for position and
conflicts over competence. It was intentional. With this technique he
systematically disorganised the upper echelons of the Reich leadership
in order to develop and further his own authority until it became a
10 despotic tyranny.[4]

Hitler believed that mere will-power was the solution to most problems. He loathed the paper-work of governmental administration and

he disliked the formality of committees in which issues could be discussed. He was not even very decisive, when it came to making a choice. Thus, although Hitler was portrayed as the all-powerful dictator, he never showed any inclination to co-ordinate government. For example, the role of the cabinet declined quite markedly after 1935. It met only four times in 1936 and the last official cabinet meeting was held in February 1938. Consequently, rivalry between the various factions of the Party and state below Hitler was rife and decision-making became more often than not the result of the Führer's whim or an informal conversation rather than rational clear-cut chains of command. This situation was exacerbated further by Hitler's lifestyle: the unusual sleeping hours; the long periods of absence from Berlin; and the tendency to become immersed in pet projects such as architectural plans. In this way Hitler's personal behaviour as dictator directly contributed to the chaotic government structure of Nazi Germany.

Historians are now generally in agreement about the confusion in Nazi government. However, there remain two very distinct schools of thought about how this should be interpreted. The so-called 'intentionalist' approach continues to uphold the absolutely vital role of Hitler in the development of the Third Reich. Consequently, the prevailing chaos is seen as a result of a deliberate policy of divide and rule on the part of Hitler – in effect an attempt (and obviously successful) to maintain his own political authority by encouraging division and confusion in both the structure and personnel of government. This, in essence, is the view outlined by Bracher and since developed further into its most overt form by Jäckel.[5] For such historians Nazism was in essence Hitlerism and all the vital developments of the Third Reich emanated from Hitler and his 'blueprint for power'. The alternative interpretation has been dubbed 'structuralist' or 'functionalist', and is expressed most forcefully in the works of Broszat and Mommsen.[6] They believe that the Nazi regime and its policies evolved from the pressure of circumstances and that the confusion in government was actually a reflection of Hitler's limitations because of the continued influence of other sources of power. Indeed, Mommsen even goes as far as to describe Hitler as 'unwilling to take decisions, frequently uncertain, exclusively concerned with upholding his prestige and personal authority, influenced in the strongest fashion by his current entourage, in some respects a weak dictator'.[7]

In the light of such contradictory claims it is clearly vital to consider in more detail those other forces before drawing any conclusions about Hitler's role in the Third Reich.

c) The Apparatus of the Police State

Amidst all the confusion of the state and Party structure there emerged an organisation which was to become the mainstay of the Third Reich – the SS. The SS developed an identity and structure of its own which kept it separate from the state and yet, through its dominance of police matters, linked it with the state.

The SS had been formed in 1925 as an elite body-guard for Hitler, but it remained a relatively minor section of the SA until Himmler became its leader in 1929. By 1933 the SS numbered 52,000, and it had established a reputation for blind obedience and total commitment to the Nazi cause. Himmler had also created in 1931 a special security service, *Sicherheitsdienst* (SD), to act as the Party's own internal police force. In the course of 1933–4 he assumed control of all the political police in the *Länder*, including the Gestapo in Prussia. Thus, Hitler turned to Himmler's SS to carry out the purge of June 1934. The loyalty and brutal efficiency of the SS on the Night of the Long Knives had its rewards, for it now became an independent organisation within the Party. Two years later all police powers were unified under Himmler's control as 'Chief of the German Police' and in 1939 all party and state police organisations were amalgamated into one by the creation of the RSHA.

As *Reichsführer SS*, Himmler controlled a massive police apparatus which was answerable only to Hitler. The SS-Police-SD system had grown into one of the key power blocs in the Third Reich. It assumed responsibility for all security matters; the concentration camps were run by its Death's Head Units; it formed its own military divisions, which were to develop into the elite fighting units of the *Waffen* SS; and increasingly it became involved in the various racial issues.

The SS-Police-SD system became in effect in the words of Kogon 'a state within a state'.[8] It was a huge vested interest, which numbered 250,000 in 1939 and had begun to eclipse other interest groups in terms of power and influence. With the onset of war this tendency was accentuated further. As German troops gained control over more and more areas of Europe, the power of the SS was inevitably enhanced. The job of internal security became much greater – by 1945 the Gestapo alone had grown to 40,000, and SS officers were granted draconian powers to crush opposition. The *Waffen* SS increased from three divisions in 1939 to 35 in 1945, so that it rivalled the power of the Army. Above all, the SS became responsible for the creation of the 'New Order' in eastern Europe (the resettlement and extermination of the various 'inferior' races). Such a scheme provided opportunities for plunder and power on a massive scale, which members of the SS exploited to the full. By the end of the war the SS had created a massive commercial combine of over 150 firms, which exploited slave labour to extract raw materials and to manufacture textiles, armaments and household goods. Nevertheless, one must guard against ascribing Orwellian-type powers to the SS. The work of Gellately has recently highlighted the limits of Gestapo policing for a state with totalitarian aspirations.[9] 40,000 Gestapo officials for the whole of the Reich meant that there was a huge reliance on public informers; in practice, it meant that a large city of ½ million was policed by just

Hitler's State by Magnus Zeller

about 40 agents. Likewise, the SS was not immune to the rivalries and arguments which typified Nazi Germany for disagreements often arose, particularly with local *gauleiters* and the governors of the occupied territories.

The SS-Police-SD system under Himmler not only preserved the Nazi regime by its brutal, repressive and often arbitrary policies of law enforcement, but gradually extended its influence into all the crucial areas of life within the Third Reich. In this way it evolved over time into the key interest group in the Third Reich.

d) The Nazi Propaganda Machine

Despite the immense power of the Nazi police apparatus, it would be simplistic to believe that the regime maintained itself in power simply by the use of brutal repression. From the moment Hitler became Chancellor, propaganda played a key part in welding together the political attitudes of the nation. As Goebbels, the new Minister of Popular Enlightenment and Propaganda, stated at his first press conference on 15 March 1933:

> 1 I view the first task of the new ministry as being to establish co-ordination between the Government and the whole people ... It is not enough for people to be more or less reconciled to our regime, to be persuaded to adopt a neutral attitude towards us, rather we want to
> 5 work on people until they have capitulated to us, until they grasp ideologically that what is happening in Germany today is not an end in itself, but a means to an end. If the means achieves the end, the means is good. Whether it always satisfies stringent aesthetic criteria or not is immaterial.

Such conviction, combined with the undoubted intelligence of Goebbels, made the Propaganda Ministry a vital cog in the Nazi machine, although the man himself never gained the political pre-eminence of Göring, of Himmler, and (latterly) of Bormann.

The two most important forms of media were the radio and the press. Goebbels (and Hitler) had always recognised the effectiveness of the spoken word over the written, and they had already begun to use the new technology during the election campaigns of 1932–3. Once in power, Goebbels efficiently brought all German broadcasting, which up until this time had been organised by the *Länder*, under Nazi control by the creation of the Reich Radio Company. Furthermore, he arranged the dismissal of 13 per cent of the staff on political and racial grounds, and their replacement by his own men. He told his broadcasters in March 1933:

> 1 We make no bones about the fact that the radio belongs to us and no one else. And we will place the radio in the service of our ideology and no other ideology will find expression here ... I am placing a major responsibility in your hands, for you have in your hands the most

5 modern instrument in existence for influencing the masses. By this
   instrument you are the creators of public opinion.

Yet, control of broadcasting was of little value in terms of propaganda
unless the people had the means to receive it, and in 1932 less than
25 per cent of German households owned a wireless. Consequently,
the government made provision for the production of a cheap set, the
Volksempfänger (People's Receiver). By 1939 70 per cent of German
homes had access to a radio – the highest national figure in the world
– and it became a medium of mass communication.

Broadcasting was also directed at public places. The installation of
loudspeakers in restaurants and cafés, factories and offices made
them all into venues for collective listening. 'Radio wardens' were
even appointed, whose duty it was to co-ordinate the listening process.

Control of the press was not so easily achieved by Goebbels.
Germany had over 4,700 daily newspapers in 1933 – a consequence of
the strong regional identities which still existed in a relatively new
nation state. Moreover, the papers were all owned privately, and traditionally owed no allegiance to central or local government; their
loyalty was to their publishing company, religious denomination or
political party. Various measures were taken to achieve Nazi control.
Firstly, the Nazi publishing house, *Eher Verlag*, bought up numerous
newspapers, so that by 1939 it controlled two-thirds of the German
press. Secondly, the various news agencies were merged into one, the
DNB; this was state controlled, with the result that news material was
vetted even before it got to the journalists. Thirdly, Goebbels introduced a daily press conference at the Propaganda Ministry to provide
guidance on editorial policy. And finally, by the so-called *Editors Law*
of October 1933, newspaper content was made the sole responsibility
of the editor; it became his job to satisfy the requirements of the
Propaganda Ministry, or face the appropriate consequences. In this
way, as one historian has explained, 'There was no need for censorship because the editor's most important function was that of censor'.

To a large extent, the Nazis succeeded in muzzling the press so that
even the internationally renowned *Frankfurter Zeitung* succumbed to
closure in 1943. However, the price of that success was the evolution
of a bland and sterile journalism, which undoubtedly contributed to
a 10 per cent decline in newspaper circulation before 1939.

Although control of the press and radio was Goebbels' major
objective, he gradually extended his influence so that film, music,
literature and art all came under the control of the Reich, though as
was shown in chapter 5 Nazi attempts to propagate a distinctive Nazi
culture were relatively unsuccessful.

One final aspect of the Goebbels propaganda machine was the
deliberate attempt to create a new kind of social ritual. The *Heil Hitler*
greeting, the Nazi salute, the *Horst Wessel* song and the preponder-
ance of militaristic uniforms were all intended to strengthen the individual's identity with the regime. This was further encouraged by the

establishment of a series of public festivals to commemorate historic days in the Nazi calendar.

Historic Days in the Nazi Calendar	
30 January	The seizure of power (1933)
24 February	Party Foundation Day (1925)
16 March	Heroes' Remembrance Day (War Dead)
20 April	Hitler's birthday
1 May	National Day of Labour
2nd Sunday in May	Mothering Sunday
Summer solstice	Pagan festival
September	Nuremberg Party rally
9 November	The Munich *putsch* (1923)
Winter solstice	Pagan festival to counter Christmas

It is extraordinarily difficult to assess how effective Nazi propaganda was in any quantitative sense. The extent of its influence clearly has massive implications for the whole thorny issue of public opinion which is considered in chapter 8. However, it is clear that the Nazi system of government directed a lot of resources towards its propaganda machine in order to glorify the regime, to inculcate its values and to integrate the nation's diverse elements. In addition it was sufficiently concerned about public morale that agents were encouraged to conduct surveys so that reports could be drawn up of popular attitudes. One such report in November 1938 read as follows:

1 There was great tension and concern everywhere and people expressed the wish that there should be no war. This was put particularly firmly by the front line fighters of the World War ... Listening in to foreign broadcasts has produced confusion and fickleness on the part
5 of the great mass of the politically uneducated. Political indoctrination and education, particularly to prepare people for war, is still completely inadequate. Only very few of the lower-ranking party leaders at present in office have achieved success with this education. One can only regard it as almost total failure.

Such reports give backing to the view that in the context of the politics of power the apparatus of propaganda and its popular impact were of secondary importance compared to the influence exerted by the apparatus of terror.

3 The Army

> **KEY ISSUE** To what extent did the German Army uphold the Nazi regime?

In any political system the role of the armed forces is vital for political stability. A regime which fails to maintain the support of the military will lack credibility in both its domestic and foreign policies. Indeed, whenever there is news of a political *coup*, it is usually the stance adopted by the military which proves to be the decisive factor in the survival or overthrow of the government.

In Germany the military tradition went back a long way into the nation's past. Above all, it was the reputation established by Prussian militarism which so often evoked comment. 'Prussia is not a country with an army: it is an army with a country,' the French statesman Mirabeau had observed in the late eighteenth century. It was the power of the Prussian military machine which had enabled Bismarck to forge German unification out of the wars with Denmark (1864), Austria (1866) and France (1870–1). Thereafter, the Army was always to be found at the centre of German political life. The military elite enjoyed great social status and the leading generals exerted considerable influence, as was shown in the intrigue of 1932–3 and in the manoeuvrings which culminated in the Night of the Long Knives. How then did the Army fit into the power structure of the Third Reich? How did Nazism, with its revolutionary and totalitarian claims, cope with such a powerful and traditional vested interest?

In the immediate aftermath of the Night of the Long Knives, it seemed as if the Army was in a position of considerable strength. Unlike other institutions, it had not been 'co-ordinated' and its leaders were confident that they had gained a certain primacy as Hitler had agreed to the destruction of his own SA. Ironically, it was even believed by many Army officers that the extremist element within Nazism had been removed and that they could now make the Nazi state work according to their interests and wishes. However, with hindsight, it is clear that although the Army had succeeded in preserving its influence in the short term, this had been achieved by a compromise which was to be fatal in the long term. This is most clearly shown by the new oath of loyalty demanded by Hitler of all soldiers, and accepted by Field Marshal von Blomberg, the Defence Minister, and General von Fritsch, the Commander-in-Chief of the Army:

> I swear by God this sacred oath: that I will render unconditional obedience to the Führer of the German Reich and people, Adolf Hitler, the Supreme Commander of the Armed Forces, and will be ready as a brave soldier to risk my life at any time for this oath.

For a German soldier, bound by discipline and obedience, such words marked a commitment which made any future resistance an act of the most serious treachery.

In the years 1934–7 the relationship between the Nazi state and the Army remained cordial. Encouraged by the rearmament programme and the reintroduction of conscription in March 1935 (thereby increasing the size of the Army to 550,000), the High Command deceived itself into believing that its pre-eminent position was being preserved. In 1935 Blomberg even issued the following decree:

1 With the introduction of conscription, the Armed Forces again became the great school of national education ... The Führer designates the completion of military service as the prerequisite for the granting of the rights of citizenship ... The educational goal of the Wehrmacht is not
5 only the basically trained soldier and the master of a weapon, but also the man who is aware of his nationality and his general attitude towards the State ... The Wehrmacht does not need to pursue prestige politics. Its best propaganda is the successful education of the youth in the spirit of National Socialism, according to the will of its supreme commander.

In fact, the power of the SS was growing fast, whilst Hitler himself had little respect for the conservative attitudes held by many officers. It was merely political realism which held him back from involvement in Army affairs until 1938.

In November 1937 Hitler had outlined at the Hossbach meeting (see page 124) his foreign policy aims of expansion. Blomberg and Fritsch, given Germany's state of military unpreparedness, were both seriously concerned by Hitler's talk of war and conquest. Their doubts only served further to convince Hitler of the spineless nature of the Army leadership, and in February 1938 both men were forced from office after revelations about their private lives. Blomberg had just married for the second time, with Hitler as principal witness, but it subsequently became known that his wife had a criminal record for theft and prostitution. Fritsch was falsely accused of homosexual offences – on evidence conveniently produced by Himmler. He wrote the following account two days before his enforced resignation:

1 On 3 January 1934 I was appointed Commander-in-Chief with effect from 1 February against the Führer's wishes, against Blomberg's wishes, but under the strongest pressure from Field Marshal von Hindenburg ... Reichenau's and the Party's struggle against me began on the day of
5 my appointment, in so far as it had not already begun ... The Party sees in me not only the man who opposed the ambitions of the SA but also tried to block the influx of party political maxims into the Army. Finally, the SS military wing, which is continually being expanded, must create conflict with the Army through its very existence. It is the living
10 proof of mistrust towards the Army and its leadership.

This rather sordid episode provided Hitler with the perfect opportunity to subordinate the Army. The post of Defence Minister was abolished, and Hitler himself became Commander-in-Chief of all armed forces with a personal high command, the *Oberkommando der Wehrmacht* (OKW), headed by a loyal adherent, General Keitel. The new Commander-in-Chief of the Army was General Brauchitsch – another compliant supporter of the regime. In addition to these changes, a further 16 generals were retired and 44 transferred.

There is little doubt that from 1938 the Army's ability to shape political developments in Germany was drastically reduced. Whereas in the early years of the Nazi regime Hitler had correctly recognised the need to work with the Army leadership, by early 1938 he was strong enough to mould it more closely to his requirements. That is not to say that the Army was without power, but merely that it had been tamed to serve its new master. Thus, it was generally recognised by the opponents of Nazism that the Army remained the one institution with the technical means of striking successfully at the regime. For example, it is now known that in the summer of 1938 a plan was drawn up by a number of disillusioned generals to arrest Hitler in the event of a full-scale European war breaking out over the Sudeten crisis. However, from 1938 to 1942 Nazi diplomatic and military policy was so successful that it effectively torpedoed the plans of those officers who wished to organise military resistance. Moreover, once Germany found itself at war again, resistance was not only treasonable, but it also smacked of a basic lack of patriotism.

By early 1943 the military situation had changed dramatically. Defeat in North Africa had been followed by the disaster of Stalingrad. Many generals came to believe that the war could not be won, and yet the Army was continuing to fight on behalf of a regime which had legitimised appalling atrocities and was now demanding 'total war'. The involvement of some leading officers in the failed 20 July Bomb Plot marked the end of the powerful and privileged position of the Army in German society (see chapter 8). Many officers were among those arrested or executed in the brutal Gestapo enquiry which followed. However, perhaps even more significant than this blood purge, were the orders subsequently issued. The Nazi salute became compulsory throughout the Army; political officers were appointed to oversee the indoctrination of the Army; and finally, with Himmler's appointment as Commander-in-Chief of the Home Army, the Army was brought under the control of the SS. The last traces of Army independence had been subsumed within the Nazi regime.

Generally, historians have not been sympathetic to the role played by the German Army during the Nazi years. Indeed, although one must avoid institutional stereotyping and recognise that there were different shades of opinion, it is difficult to avoid the conclusion that the Army leadership played a naive and inept political game. Conditioned by their traditions of obedience, loyalty and patriotism, and encouraged by the authoritarian disposition of the Third Reich, the Army became a vital mainstay of the Nazi regime in the early years. Yet, even when its own power to influence events had been drastically reduced in 1938 and the full implications of Nazi rule became apparent during the war, the Army's leaders could not escape from their political and moral dilemma. The 20 July plot was a brave gesture, but the vacillation and indecision of that day were also indicative of the compromised position in which the Army found itself by this time.

4 Big Business

> **KEY ISSUE** How influential was big business in the Third Reich?

The position of big business in the Third Reich has long been a focus of interest. Many on the political left have viewed Nazism as a tool of capitalism which used the Nazi state for its own sake and in that sense dominated the power structure in the Third Reich. (See chapter 9 for a explanation of the Marxist interpretation.) Although such a generalised theoretical explanation was never accepted as an orthodoxy, it is only lately, as a result of some detailed research into a number of firms and industries, that a real picture is beginning to emerge of the relationship between big business and the Nazi regime. We have already seen in chapter 4 that the German economy went through a number of distinct phases and this was reflected in the relationship. It would also be wrong to see big business as a uniform interest group – there were a number of different sectors and each one was affected by the changing circumstances within that twelve-year period.

From 1933 the position of the business community began to improve. Helped by the upturn in world trade, and encouraged by the Nazi destruction of the free trade unions, a commercial recovery was set in motion. However, despite all the Nazi electoral promises, small business found itself being squeezed out by the power of big business, whose support was more crucial in the creation of new jobs. Consequently, it was initially the building and the giant coal and steel industries which prospered most; whilst consumer goods production remained relatively depressed. It is therefore probably fair to say that in the first few years of Nazi rule big business was able to exert an influence and to maintain a privileged autonomy in its own sphere, just as the Army generals did in the military field.

The introduction of the Four Year Plan in 1936 marks an important turning-point. The coalition of interests between generals, business and the state disintegrated as a result of the economic crisis (see page 56) and this led to a 'far-reaching transformation of the economic power structure and hence a change in the relationship between economics and politics, industry and the state'.[10] Schacht and the leaders of heavy industry urged a curtailment of rearmament and an increased emphasis on consumer goods and exports – this was a fatal error of judgement which brought about the downfall of Schacht and the end of heavy industry's supremacy. Instead, Göring, as director of the Four Year Plan, was now able to call the shots and the only groups able to maintain any semblance of real influence were in the electrochemicals sector because of their crucial role in rearmament; in the chemical industry IG Farben led the way with its development of synthetic substitutes, whilst the electrical industry was dominated by Siemens. Most telling of all was the subservience of the Ruhr barons of heavy industry – when they refused to co-operate Göring national-ised the iron-ore deposits and created a new state firm, the *Reichswerke Hermann Göring*, to exploit them. From 1936 the divisions and weak-nesses in big business meant that the needs of the economy were determined by political decisions, especially those in foreign and mili-tary policy. Private property always remained in private hands, but the free market and business independence gave way to state regulation and coercion. On the whole business therefore accepted the primacy of politics, fearful that resistance to state interference would only exacerbate the situation further.

Business had little to gain from a general European war in 1939 and its fears were soon confirmed. Access to the new markets of the conquered territories was not enough to offset the loss of overseas trade and the general economic disruption of war. More telling in political terms was the subjugation of business to even greater con-trols and direction from the state and the military, which fatally com-promised Germany's war production in the early years. Of course, from 1942 Speer's reforms liberated business to some extent, but it was still forced to operate within a political framework and the prior-ities were clearly set by the regime. Thus, to the very end German industry continued to work with the regime. There was no real oppo-sition to the brutal use of forced labour and leaders of big business were not to be found amongst the plotters of July 1944. Perhaps this was because the material benefits were on the whole just too attrac-tive. Profits generally continued to increase until the end of the war and this was reason enough to work with the regime. However, that is not say that they ever directed policy. From 1936 this was clearly deter-mined by the Nazi leadership:

> German business can be likened to the conductor of a runaway bus, who has no control over the actions of the driver, but keeps collecting the passengers' fares right up to the final crash.[11]

5 Conclusion: the Third Reich – a Polycratic Regime?

> **KEY ISSUES** What is meant by the term 'polycracy'? In what ways could the Third Reich be described as such a regime?

To describe the Third Reich as 'totalitarian' is not inaccurate. However, it is possibly misleading as it is a term which is a product of the Cold War, when liberal Western historians rather too readily assumed an identity between Hitler's Germany, Stalin's Russia and Mussolini's Italy. Even more dubious was the attempt by Soviet histo-rians to portray the Nazi state as simply the political manifestation of a powerful capitalist elite. Both interpretations have become inadequate explanations of the power structure in the Third Reich.

The totalitarian model of Nazi Germany can be criticised on two major counts. Although Germany was politically a one-party state, the Nazi Party did not have the organisation or unity of purpose to dominate affairs (unlike the Communists in the USSR). Secondly, the Nazis never established a centralised command control over the economy (in direct contrast to the situation in USSR). Nazi Germany was not the monolithic structure suggested by the term totalitarian. Equally, however, the continued existence of private enterprise and the obvious sympathy of certain elements of big business for the regime in no way amounts to an acceptance of the traditional Marxist view. For, in reality, it is only possible to sustain the thesis that economic forces predominated at the expense of other power blocs by ignoring much of the available evidence.

Instead, historians have increasingly come to the view that the Third Reich in its power structure was a 'polycracy' – an alliance of different blocs, which, although not in unison, were dependent on each other and prepared to work with each other as partners in power. The most important of these blocs would seem to have been the Nazi Party itself, the SS-Police-SD system, the Army, big business and, to some extent, the higher levels of the state bureaucracy (although even this picture is over-simplified and disguises the divisions and conflicts within these various groups). At the centre of all this there was the looming presence of Hitler himself.

However, even this picture is too basic, since the relationship between these 'power blocs' was far from static. In the early years, Hitler and the Nazis – at this stage the SS-Police-SD system was relatively insignificant – were heavily dependent upon the sympathy of the Army and big business, and so they did not attempt to control them directly because they feared alienating them. Indeed, the destruction of the SA in 1934 was motivated very much by the need to placate the traditional vested interests, and it was seen as a blow by many in the Party. At this stage, the rearmament programme also acted as a powerful focus of common interest – contracts and profits for industry, restored prestige for the Army, and foundations being laid for the future imperial expansion planned by the Nazis.

All this changed in the course of 1936–8. Hitler's personal political position was by this time much stronger and was ruthlessly supported by the emerging power of Himmler's SS-Police-SD system. Hitler was therefore less constrained by the need for political compromise and could afford to pursue his objectives more directly. Consequently, the economic crisis of 1936 led to the disappearance of Schacht and the introduction of the Four Year Plan under Göring intended to create a war economy. This development represented a major shift in the balance of power away from big business as a whole, although it was strongly supported by the electro-chemicals sector because of its links with arms production. Despite the fact that the Army had sided with the Nazi leadership in 1936, it was also severely weakened two years later by the purge of major generals after Blomberg and Fritsch had expressed their doubts about the direction of Hitler's foreign policy.

By 1938, therefore, both the Army and big business had been reduced to the role of junior partners in the Third Reich's power structure. This weakening of their positions was to continue in subsequent years, although at first the Army gained great kudos from the military victories of 1939–41. However, it was under the pressures of war that the power and influence of the SS-Police-SD system was able to grow so enormously and to become the dominant power bloc – so much so that some historians have gone so far as to refer to the emergence of the 'SS state'. This also coincided with the weakening of the traditional elites within the state bureaucracy as the Party apparatus under Bormann's influence began to exert a relatively greater influence. It would seem therefore that by the time of the Third Reich's eventual demise the various organs of Nazism had progressively assumed a more and more dominant role to the detriment of external agencies.

Structuralist historians have certainly succeeded in highlighting a lack of planning and organisation on Hitler's part, so that it is now generally appreciated that divisions and rivalries in the government of the Third Reich persisted throughout its twelve-year life. Both Himmler and Göring headed their own institutional empires and their aims and interests often brought them into conflict not only with each other, but also with other leading Nazis. Likewise, Speer and Sauckel (Minister for Labour) clashed continuously over the direction of labour in the war economy, whilst Bormann and Goebbels were both so despised within the Party that personal rivalries and ambitions often dominated at the expense of efficient government. Yet, despite all this talk of individual and institutional confrontation, it is difficult to ignore Hitler or to accept the view of him as a 'weak dictator' (except perhaps in the last few months of his life). Hitler created the Party and headed a regime which was built upon the principle of authoritarian leadership. It is impossible to pin-point any major domestic development which was contrary to Hitler's wishes. Equally, it was Hitler's own views on continental conquest and racial supremacy which determined Germany's foreign and military policy. In the final analysis, it is surely indicative that the SS-Police-SD complex emerged as *the* dominant power bloc and its guiding principle from the start had been unquestioning obedience to the will of the *Führer*.

References

1 C.J. Friedrich & Z. Brzezinski, *Totalitarian Dictatorship and Autocracy* (Camb. Mass., 1956)

2 E. Huber. Quoted in J. Noakes & G. Pridham, *Nazism 1919–45: a documentary reader* Vol. 2, (Exeter, 1983) p. 198

3 F. Wiedemann. Quoted in Noakes & Pridham op. cit. Vol. 2 p. 207–8

4 O. Dietrich. Quoted in Noakes & Pridham op. cit. Vol. 2 p. 205

5 See K.D. Bracher, *The German Dictatorship* (Penguin, 1973) E. Jäckel, *Hitler's Weltanschauung; A Blueprint for Power* (Middletown Conn., 1972)

6 See M. Broszat, *The Hitler State* (Engl. trans. 1981, London) and H. Mommsen, *From Weimar to Auschwitz* (Engl. trans. 1991, Oxford)

7 H. Mommsen. Quoted in I. Kershaw, *The Nazi Dictatorship* (3rd ed, London, 1993) p. 60

8 See E. Kogon, *The Theory and Practice of Hell* (Engl. trans., Secker & Warburg, 1950)

9 See R. Gellately, *The Gestapo and German Society. Enforcing Racial Policy* (Oxford, 1990)

10 T.W. Mason, 'Politics and Economics in National Socialist Germany' in S.J. Woolf, *The Nature of Fascism* (London, 1968) p. 178

11 R. Grunberger, *A Social History of the Third Reich* (Penguin, 1974) p. 184

Summary Diagram
The political structure of the Third Reich

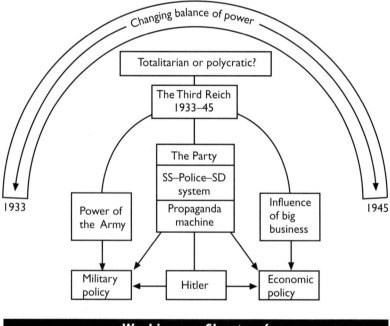

Working on Chapter 6

The content of this chapter is pivotal. It builds on your knowledge and understanding of chapters 3, 4 and 5 and it also makes reference to the material to be covered in chapters 7 and 8. First, it is most important for you to gain a good overview of the political system. One way of doing this would be to draw the summary diagram and to memorise its key elements. Secondly, you must try to appreciate that the political balance of powers changed over time. You could do this as a group activity with each individual taking responsibility for one interest group and then reporting back on its strengths and weaknesses. At the end, though, you must have a detailed set of notes for each section so that you fully appreciate when and why each element did or did not exert power and/or influence. Make certain you include the key facts/events to back up your general statements. You might also like to express your understanding in a diagrammatic version of your own which conveys these changes across time (a graph?). Finally, to bring everything together try to summarise section 5 in no more than 200 words.

Answering structured and essay questions on Chapter 6

In this chapter you have looked at the political structure of the Third Reich in its broadest sense, although doing this has involved a fairly detailed examination of certain key elements. It is important for you to have a good basic knowledge of all those elements because you can then choose the appropriate facts and apply them as required. Look at the following structured questions:

1. **a)** What was the position of the following in the power structure of the Third Reich: the SS; German big business; the apparatus of propaganda?
    b) Explain why some historians argue that Hitler was not 'master in the Third Reich'.
2. **a)** Outline the relationship between the German Army and the Nazi state in the years 1933–45.
    b) Would you agree that the German Army became a 'vital mainstay of the regime'?

Clearly, the first part in each question directs you towards what is required. But even then there is an implication to explain as well as a prescribed element to be described. In the second part of each question you have again been given a focus. But you should also treat it as a prompt to think broadly. In 1b) you should draw attention not only to Hitler's perceived weaknesses of leadership, but also to the other forces at work counteracting his power and influence. In 2b) you can explain why the Army's support was so important, but you should also highlight the divisions and doubts within it and also refer to its importance relative to other crucial elements.

In essay questions it is much more likely that you will be confronted with questions inviting a broad analysis of the Nazi state. Many of these questions will fall into the 'to what extent' category. Although such questions may be phrased with a point of focus, they all require you to construct a two-part answer. The first part will examine the points in favour of the proposition and the second part will discuss those against it. Consider these questions:

1. To what extent would you agree with the description of the Third Reich as the 'SS state'?
2. To what extent was the Party the most vital element in the Nazi state?
3. How far did the Nazis change the political structure of Germany?
4. To what extent was Nazi Germany controlled by the dictatorial leadership of Adolf Hitler?
5. To what extent was the Third Reich built upon the use of political terror?
6. How valid is the term 'totalitarian' as a description of the Third Reich?

Each of these questions requires you to weigh the significance of the proposition against the other contributory factors. For example, question 2 asks you to assess the importance of the Party in the Nazi state, so by implication you must also analyse other 'elements' in order to reach a conclusion. What other elements would you need to discuss? Remember that the majority of your time should be devoted to a consideration of the importance of the Party.

Now prepare an essay plan for question 4 based around the following sub-questions:

a) In what ways did Hitler exert control in the Third Reich?
b) In what ways did he fail to exert control?
c) Who/what also exerted control?

Finally, write out your conclusion in full. This will be a difficult task if it is done properly because you will be trying to integrate all the evidence into a crisp and coherent statement. However, doing it will certainly help to clarify your thoughts on the topic.

Source-based questions on Chapter 6

1. The Role of Hitler

Read the extracts on pages 99–100 about Hitler's constitutional position; his daily routine; and his style of leadership. Answer the following questions:

a) What major political failings are highlighted in the description of Hitler's lifestyle? (4 marks)
b) According to Huber, what was the nature and theory of the Führer's power and why do you think the regime went to the trouble of producing such verbose constitutional theory? (5 marks)
c) Why do you think the position of Führer was not portrayed as a state office? (3 marks)
d) How far does Dietrich support the view expressed by Wiedemann about Hitler's style of leadership? (5 marks)
e) How far do these documents and other evidence known to you support

the view that the Third Reich was actually led by a weak dictator? (*8 marks*)

2. Nazi Attitudes to Propaganda

Read the two extracts from Goebbels on pages 104 and 105 and the report on page 106. Answer the following questions:

a) Explain in your own words Goebbels' major aims as Minister of Propaganda. (*4 marks*)

b) Why did Goebbels place so much importance on the control of the radio? (*3 marks*)

c) How reliable is the report as evidence of popular attitudes in 1938? (*5 marks*)

d) Would you agree that the regime's attempts at political indoctrination were 'an almost total failure'? (*8 marks*)

3. The Role of the Army

Study the military oath and the statements by Blomberg and Fritsch on pages 107–8. Answer the following questions:

a) Explain the following references:
   (i) 'under the strongest pressure from Field Marshal von Hindenburg' (page 108 line 3) (*1 mark*)
   (ii) 'the SS military wing, which is continually being expanded' (page 108 line 8) (*1 mark*)

b) Explain the significance of the new military oath and the circumstances in which it was issued. (*3 marks*)

c) What was the role of the armed forces in Nazi Germany according to Blomberg? (*4 marks*)

d) How reliable is Fritsch's account as an analysis of relations between the Army and the Nazi Party in the years 1934 to 1938? (*4 marks*)

e) 'The German Army remained loyal to the Nazi regime until it became clear that the war was lost.' Do these sources and other evidence known to you support this view? (*7 marks*)

4. The Structure of the Third Reich

Study the painting by Zeller on page 103 and the poster on the front cover. Answer the following questions:

a) What impression of Hitler is the artist trying to create in the poster? Explain your answer. (*4 marks*)

b) How accurately does the poster's slogan reflect Nazi ideology? (*5 marks*)

c) Zeller's painting was entitled 'Hitler's State'. What is the image of the Third Reich as projected by the artist? (*7 marks*)

d) Despite the differences what similarities can you detect in the way the two sources portray the structure of the Third Reich? (*4 marks*)

7 The Rise and Fall of the Third Reich

POINTS TO CONSIDER

Although this book is essentially concerned with the impact of Nazism upon the domestic history of Germany, the student of the Third Reich cannot ignore the issue of foreign policy and Germany's position in the international community. It would be wrong to treat domestic and foreign issues in isolation from each other, because in the case of Nazi Germany they are so clearly inter-related. It should also be borne in mind that the coverage of the topic in this chapter is only partial and inevitably focuses on Germany's role (albeit a very important one) in events between 1933 and 1945. For a more rounded discussion of international relations in the inter-war period it would be a good idea to consult the companion volume in this series, *War and Peace: International Relations, 1919–45*. Nevertheless, there is still a lot of detail in this chapter and you must be careful not to get too lost in it during your first reading. Above all, you should try to: a) identify and understand the main chronological phases and b) recognise why certain events are identified as turning-points.

KEY DATES

1933	**Oct**	Germany withdrew from League of Nations and Disarmament Conference.
1935	**March**	Reintroduction of military conscription.
1936	**March**	Remilitarisation of Rhineland by German troops.
1937	**Nov**	Hitler's address to chiefs of armed services – the so-called Hossbach Conference.
1938	**March**	*Anschluss* with Austria.
	Sept	Munich agreement ceded Sudetenland to Germany.
1939	**Mar**	Invasion of Czechoslovakia: Munich agreement undone and self-determination ignored.
	Aug	Nazi–Soviet Pact.
	1 Sept	German invasion of Poland.
1941	**June**	'Operation Barbarossa' – German invasion of USSR.
	Dec	German declaration of war on USA following Pearl Harbor: continental war 'globalised'.
1943	**Jan**	German surrender at Stalingrad.
1944	**June**	Allied landings in Normandy.
1945	**May**	German surrender: division of Germany.

1 The Framework of Nazi Foreign Policy

> **KEY ISSUES** What was the historical context for the development
> of Nazi foreign policy? How have the aims of Nazi foreign policy
> been interpreted by historians?

Despite the impositions and restraints of the Treaty of Versailles, and
despite the dire economic condition of the country in 1933, Germany
was able to pursue a major continental war within seven years of
Hitler's assumption of power. This apparently remarkable transformation in her fortunes was largely made possible by the continental balance of power which had prevailed since 1918. The great empires of
Russia, Austria-Hungary and Turkey had gone for ever, creating a
power vacuum in central and eastern Europe which could not be
filled by a weak and isolated USSR, by the generally unstable suc-
cessor states to the Habsburg empire, or by a modernising and
inward-looking Turkish republic. Moreover, Britain and France had
been decisively weakened by the effects of total war, whilst the USA
had retreated into isolation and showed little inclination to uphold
the European order which it had done so much to create between
1917 and 1919. In such a situation, the recovery of Germany with its
vast economic potential and manpower, was always likely. Indeed, the
revision of the Versailles settlement and the re-emergence of
Germany as a great power had already begun under the Weimar
Republic. What then were to be the aims of Nazi foreign policy?

In the decade after the Nuremberg trials of 1945–6 it was widely
assumed that the expansionist aims of Nazi foreign policy dated from
1937. Hitler's address to the service chiefs and the Foreign Minister in
November of that year, which was recorded in the so-called Hossbach
Memorandum, seemed to mark the turning-point from a revisionist
(i.e., attempting to revise the terms of the Treaty of Versailles) policy to
one of aggressive expansion. Such a view is not now generally accepted.

As far back as 1960 the English historian Hugh Trevor-Roper, in
his article 'Hitler's War Aims', drew attention to the systematic nature
of Hitler's ideas on foreign policy from the very outset of his political
career. Such an interpretation has been more fully developed by the
so-called 'programme' school of historians (intentionalists) in
Germany. In their view, Hitler had a clearly defined set of objectives,
which amounted to a 'stage by stage plan' (*Stufenplan*). However,
there remain conflicting opinions over the precise extent of his
ambitions. The 'continentalists' believe that planned expansion was
to be limited to the establishment of a hegemony within Europe. The
'globalists' go further and support the thesis that Hitler aspired to
German supremacy in the Middle East and Africa (in particular, at
the expense of British colonial territories) and finally to a struggle
with the USA for world domination.[1]

The 'programme' school has established an unusually high degree of acceptance within academic circles. Even the dispute between the 'globalists' and the 'continentalists' is rather contrived – since it does not revolve around what actually happened, but around the significance that can be accorded to some rather vague statements from Hitler himself on Germany's future world role. Yet, on essentials both interpretations are in agreement: they uphold the central place of Hitler himself in the creation of Nazi foreign policy; they emphasise the racialist framework of that foreign policy; and they view the conquest of *Lebensraum* as the basis upon which Hitler intended to build German status as a great power.

If many historians now accept the concept of some kind of Hitler 'programme', divisions of interptetation do manifest themselves more obviously over the analysis of the actual events between 1933 and 1945. Whereas the 'intentionalists' maintain that Hitler's character and programme were the key factors in the shaping of German foreign policy, opponents in the 'structuralist' school have pinpointed other forces at work. In particular, supporters of the polycratic view of the Third Reich see all aspects of policy, including foreign policy, being shaped by numerous agencies and institutions, both inside and outside the Party. Some deny that there was any consistency. They see merely a confused variety of aims – 'expansion without object'. One historian even goes as far as to suggest that Hitler's goals were 'utopian' and that it was the dynamism of the Nazi movement, with its incessant demands for change which transformed *Lebensraum* from an 'ideological metaphor' into political reality.[2] Another point of view relates the evolution of Nazi foreign policy to the domestic economic pressures building up in the second half of the 1930s (see also chapter 4). It is suggested that it was the need to overcome internal discontent created by the constraints of Nazi economic policy which shaped Nazi foreign policy. In order to preserve his own political supremacy at home, Hitler was forced to accelerate his war-like ambitions.[3]

Such attempts to portray Nazi foreign policy and strategy as the instruments of social forces have not threatened the established position of the 'programme' school. However, they do underline the need to be careful of imposing too much order and regularity on our historical explanations of Nazi foreign policy by utilising the benefits of hindsight. Secondly, they correctly draw attention to the dangers of Hitler-centred interpretations. The determining forces in any country's foreign policy are many. Even a dictator such as Hitler was not immune from circumstance and extra-personal factors. However, the ultimate direction of Nazi policy was undoubtedly a reflection of Hitler's personal ideological framework. In that sense, one can speak of *Hitler's* foreign policy.

2 The Revisionist Phase, 1933–7

> **KEY ISSUES** What is meant by a revisionist foreign policy? How did Nazi foreign policy manage to break free of Germany's weak international position in the early years of the regime?

a) The Beginnings of Nazi Foreign Policy

Hitler's appointment as Chancellor did not immediately usher in a new era in German foreign policy. Indeed, the post of foreign minister remained in the hands of Constantin von Neurath, a conservative nationalist, which suggested continuity rather than change. Such a public perception suited Hitler. Economic and military circumstances demanded a cautious approach: Germany's unemployment had just peaked at 6.1 million and its Army was still limited to 100,000 men. Moreover, the priority was the establishment of dictatorship at home rather than grandiose diplomatic escapades abroad. Consequently, in the early years of Nazi foreign policy, Hitler's objectives were limited to the cultivation of friendship with Britain and Italy to avoid Germany's isolation, and to the weakening of French power and influence wherever possible.

Hitler was helped in this by the changing international situation, which was moving in Germany's favour. The Japanese invasion of Manchuria in 1931 had not only highlighted the ineffectiveness of the League of Nations, but had also underlined the strategic dilemma facing Britain: namely, how could it uphold the global commitments to its Empire, act as 'world policeman' for the League, and also play a major role in the defence of the European *status quo*. The severity of the Depression had already driven the USA further into isolation; whilst in France its effects, although felt later, were to contribute to the destabilisation of the political system and thereby pave the way for a lack of consistent resolve in foreign affairs.

However, the need for caution in this first phase of Nazi foreign policy was also effectively exploited, for it enabled the regime to appear to be reasonable and to lull many within Europe into a false sense of security. This was exemplified by Germany's withdrawal from the Disarmament Conference and the League of Nations in 1933, following France's refusal to accept parity in land forces. In this way it appeared as if the French were the unreasonable party, whilst Hitler had successfully evoked sympathy, especially from Britain and Italy (his two prospective allies). Similar benefits accrued from the unexpected signing of a ten-year non-aggression pact with Poland in January 1934. Not only did it create a favourable impression of reasonableness in international diplomatic circles, but it also falsely suggested to the Poles that an accommodation with Nazi Germany was possible. However, the pact's significance went further than mere propaganda; it effectively breached the French system of alliances in eastern Europe, and, in the short term, secured Germany's eastern flank while diplomatic problems were being dealt with in the south and west. In the long term, of course, Hitler did not envisage any place for an independent Poland – it served merely as the gateway to the creation of *Lebensraum* in the east.

Such successes did not result in any kind of formal agreement with Britain and Italy in the course of 1934. Although Britain showed considerable sympathy with Germany's revisionist demands, sympathy could not be equated with a military or strategic understanding, and several high-level diplomatic missions failed to achieve any kind of breakthrough. An alliance with Italy also seemed a long way off. The attempted *coup* by Austrian Nazis in July 1934 probably enjoyed only moral support from Berlin, but it frightened Mussolini into deploying 40,000 troops to the Austro-Italian frontier, since he regarded Austria as an important buffer-state between Germany and Italy. This incident was a clear indication of the limits of Nazi power at this time.

By the end of 1934 Hitler had secured his domestic position and the economy was recovering rapidly. His prestige was further enhanced in January 1935 when the Saarland, which for the last fifteen years had been under the control of the League of Nations, voted in a free and fair plebiscite to return to German rule. It represented a great propaganda success for the Nazis. However, if Hitler was to loosen the shackles of Versailles unilaterally, it seemed that he would require greater military power than was permitted by the treaty. Therefore, it is a reflection of Hitler's great diplomatic skills that within two years the Versailles treaty was effectively dead and the continental balance of power had shifted in favour of Germany without a single shot being fired.

b) Breaking Free from Versailles

Germany's announcement in March 1935 of the existence of a *Luftwaffe*, followed shortly afterwards by the introduction of conscription and a peace-time army of 550,000, went directly against the terms of the Treaty of Versailles and led to a combined verbal condemnation by Britain, France and Italy – the so-called Stresa Declaration. Partly in response to Allied concern, Hitler spoke to the Reichstag about the futility of war just a few weeks later, on 21 May.

i The blood shed on the European continent in the course of the last 300 years bears no proportion to the national result of the events ... What dynastic egoism, political passion and patriotic blindness have attained in the way of apparently far-reaching political changes by shedding rivers
5 of blood has, as regards national feeling, done no more than touched the skin of the nations ... If these states had applied merely a fraction of their sacrifices to wiser purposes the success would certainly have been greater and more permanent.

It was in this uncertain international atmosphere that in June 1935 Britain and Germany signed a naval agreement which ignored the terms of the Versailles treaty and allowed Germany to have a navy 35 per cent of the strength of the British fleet. Hitler had successfully detached Britain from the Stresa Front and had laid the basis for a fundamental Anglo-German understanding – or so he believed.

In the autumn of 1935 Mussolini ordered the invasion of Abyssinia (also known as Ethiopia), one of the two remaining independent African states. This destroyed the last vestiges of unity between Britain, France and Italy. When it became clear that the aggressor was to be allowed to triumph, it also underlined the impotence of the League of Nations in major international incidents. Furthermore, it created an atmosphere of crisis, which focused Anglo-French diplomacy on Italy and on threats to the world order outside of Europe. In this situation Hitler seized the initiative and ordered his troops to re-occupy the demilitarised Rhineland in March 1936. It was a bold gamble which did not enjoy the full support of the High Command or the Foreign Ministry. They believed that the risk of military retaliation was too great. Such pessimists were proved wrong and Hitler was proved right. France showed no decisive inclination to intervene and Britain was frankly indifferent. Condemnation was limited to verbal protests, more directed at Hitler's methods than at his aims. With hindsight, it is clear that the remilitarisation of the Rhineland was a decisive turning-point in European international relations in the years 1933–9. In diplomatic terms, not only the Versailles treaty but also the Locarno pacts had been overturned. Most significantly, the strategic advantage of the demilitarised buffer between France and Germany had been lost completely. French military thinking had reflected the inertia of its political leadership. It had been shown to be purely defensive and clearly incapable of taking any kind of aggressive military initiative east of the Maginot Line, the series of fortifications along France's border with Germany.

In addition, Hitler's personal standing within Germany had been enormously enhanced. One journalist later commented on the subsequent plebiscite on the remilitarisation.

1 99 per cent of the 45,453,691 registered voters went to the polls, and 98.8 per cent of them approved Hitler's action. Foreign correspondents who visited the polling stations found some irregularities ... Nevertheless, this observer, who covered the 'election' from one
5 corner of the Reich to the other, has no doubt that the vote of approval for Hitler's *coup* was overwhelming. And why not? The junking of Versailles and the appearance of German soldiers marching again into what was, after all, German territory were things that almost all Germans naturally approved.[4]

The diplomatic pendulum continued to swing in Germany's favour during 1936. A civil war broke out in Spain. This caused further political uncertainty, which was exacerbated by the military intervention of Italy, Germany and the USSR. Britain and France, fearing that the war could provide the spark for a major international conflict, struggled to maintain a policy of non-intervention. All this suited Hitler's purpose, for attention was again directed away from central Europe. It also provided a common focus for Italian and German interests which culminated in the emergence of the Rome–Berlin Axis in November 1936 – a *rapprochement* based on political, economic and ideological co-operation, although not yet extending to a military alliance.

By the end of 1936 Germany's international status had undergone a remarkable transformation. France's previously dominant position on the continent had withered away and the diplomatic and military initiative had passed to Germany. The shackles of Versailles and Locarno had been struck off at no cost. Moreover, Germany was no longer isolated – Mussolini had been detached from France and Britain and was moving ever closer to an understanding with Hitler.

c) Plans for War?

However, Hitler's position was not without problems, especially since political and economic developments within Germany impinged so heavily on the evolution of his foreign policy (hence the danger of considering each in isolation). In the autumn of 1936 the economic crisis had revealed the fragility of Germany's economic expansion (see page 57). Hitler was not yet in a position to risk fighting a war; hence the establishment of the Four Year Plan under Göring to create a war economy. There was also the problem of conservative forces in the Army and the foreign ministry. Certain elements in both these institutions had already advised a more cautious policy. If Hitler wished to raise the diplomatic stakes higher, he needed guaranteed support from such quarters. Finally, there remained the problem of securing an alliance with Britain. This had not materialised, and voices within the Party were promoting alternative diplomatic strategies. In particular, Ribbentrop, a leading and influential Nazi who operated his own personal 'bureau', was keen to develop a tripartite understanding between Germany, Japan and Italy at the expense of Britain. Hitler was not convinced, despite the developing co-operation between the three powers, and he remained wedded to the idea of the British alliance as a way of securing his long-term aim of crushing the USSR. Ironically, he sent Ribbentrop to London as Germany's new ambassador in the autumn of 1936 with the specified objective of securing an agreement with Britain.

It would seem that these problems provide a partial explanation of the relative inactivity of 1937, which clearly stands out as a dividing-line between the diplomatic coups of 1935–6 and the pre-war crises of 1938–9. However, in November 1937 at the so-called Hossbach Conference (named after Hitler's adjutant who took the surviving notes), Hitler addressed Foreign Minister Neurath, War Minister Blomberg and the three Commanders-in-Chief. The significance of the meeting has become the focus of considerable controversy. It was used by the prosecution at the Nuremberg trials and by some post-war historians to suggest that from this point 'the die was cast. Hitler had communicated his irrevocable decision to go to war'[5]. At the other extreme it has been dismissed as simply a manoeuvre in domestic affairs to overcome the conservatives' doubts about the pace of re-armament. Hitler's ideas were 'in large part day-dreaming unrelated to what followed in real life ... There was here no concrete plan, no directive for German policy in 1937 and 1938'.[6] It is likely that the pressures of competing interest groups at home did prompt Hitler's statement and, certainly, events did not unfold as outlined in Hitler's scenarios – so the document does not provide a blue-print for Nazi foreign policy. However, it would be wrong simply to dismiss its con-tents out of hand, for it does show how Hitler's policy was changing from one centred on diplomatic initiatives to one where military force was to play a much greater part. Such a view is substantiated by two sub-sequent developments. Firstly, the restructuring of the Army's High Command and the appointment of Ribbentrop as Foreign Minister, following further criticisms by Blomberg and Neurath about the dan-gers posed by the 'militarisation' of foreign policy: and secondly, the decision to develop an offensive war plan against Czechoslovakia.

3 The Road to War 1938–9

> **KEY ISSUE** Why did the diplomatic triumphs of 1938–9 culminate in war in September 1939?

a) The *Anschluss*

Whatever doubts remain about the interpretation of the Hossbach Memorandum, it did make clear that Hitler's next objectives were to be Austria and Czechoslovakia. Austria's independence was guaran-teed by the Versailles treaty. More practically, its position had been protected by Mussolini's desire to maintain a pro-Italian buffer on his northern frontier. However, by early 1938 the Austrian Nazi move-ment had re-established itself as a powerful and disruptive force fol-lowing the failed *putsch* of 1934, while Mussolini's growing friendship with Hitler suggested that an accommodation over Austria would be possible. Hitler was hopeful that diplomatic pressure and internal disruption could bring about a peaceful *Anschluss*. When the Austrian Chancellor tried to counter such a possibility by organising a national referendum, Hitler was forced into a rushed and poorly-executed invasion of Austria in March 1938 (this was technically legitimised by a Nazi dictated 'invitation' given by the Austrian government).

The *Anschluss* with Austria represented a spectacular foreign policy triumph for Hitler, after a period of relative inactivity, although an alternative perspective was provided by the SPD in exile:

1   … In these reports we have often expressed the view that Hitler can count on the support of the majority of the people in two essential respects: (1) he has created work and (2) he has made Germany strong. The further the crisis recedes into the past the more the first point will
5   lose its attraction and the more the dictatorship will rely on support for its foreign policy line. The regime simply could not let slip such a favourable opportunity as the annexation of Austria for a general attempt to justify its policy.
     Undoubtedly, the great majority of the German people was prepared
10 to approve the question posed in the plebiscite about the 'Reunification of Austria with the German Reich'. But the dictatorship cannot rest content with a majority, not even with a large majority. After the result of the last plebiscite was announced as 98.8 per cent, this time it could not be any less; it had to be more. The dictatorship feels itself to be so
15 weak that it could not bear it if it was only 97 per cent. Thus the dictatorship becomes a prisoner of its own methods.

In diplomatic terms the *Anschluss* had again shown Britain and France to be impotent or unwilling to stand up to Germany, whilst Mussolini had acquiesced in the loss of his Austrian buffer for the sake of German friendship. There were also economic advantages for the Third Reich – Austria's gold reserves and mineral deposits of iron-ore, copper and lead were of great value in the light of Germany's recurring balance of payment problems. Most importantly, Hitler had successfully overturned the strategic balance of power in central Europe. The western half of Czechoslovakia was now encircled, and control of the Danube valley from Vienna provided a gateway into south-eastern Europe.

b) Czechoslovakia

Having gained such a dramatic triumph over Austria, Hitler's attention turned almost immediately towards Czechoslovakia. The Czech crisis was to last almost a year and was to bring Europe very close to war. No clearer indication of Hitler's preparedness to use military force by this time can be found than his statement, written at the beginning of the military plan for the attack on the Czechs: 'It is my unalterable decision to smash Czechoslovakia by military action in the near future'. Of course, the existence of 3½ million Sudeten Germans in the border region of Czechoslovakia, actively stirred up by the propaganda of the Nazi Sudeten German Party, provided the perfect method of undermining the Czech state from within. While the behaviour of Britain and France (despite the fact that the latter had a mutual assistance pact with Czechoslovakia dating from 1924)

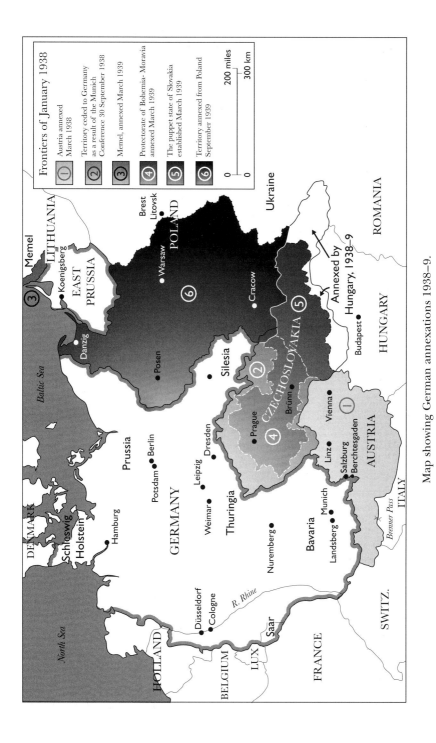

Frontiers of January 1938

① Austria annexed
March 1938

② Territory ceded to Germany
as a result of the Munich
Conference 30 September 1938

③ Memel, annexed March 1939

④ Protectorate of Bohemia–Moravia
annexed March 1939

⑤ The puppet state of Slovakia
established March 1939

⑥ Territory annexed from Poland
September 1939

0   200 miles

0   300 km

Map showing German annexations 1938–9.

suggested that they would not interfere militarily in any territorial readjustments in the region. Hitler may not have been able to secure the desired alliance with Britain, but the diplomatic messages coming out of London convinced him that the government there was prepared to write off Czechoslovakia for the sake of peace.

However, when the crisis came to a head in September 1938 – with constant clashes between Sudeten Germans and Czechs, with German and Czech troops poised on their respective frontiers and with the possibility of Britain and France being dragged into the war – Hitler settled for a diplomatic solution by accepting the Munich Agreement, which ceded only the Sudetenland to Germany. The whole incident was portrayed as another success for the Führer. Certainly, it completely cut the ground from under the feet of those generals who had been planning to arrest Hitler if war broke out. Yet, Hitler himself was far from pleased that his 'entry into Prague had been spoilt'. He had been aiming to destroy the Czech state in its entirety, but he backed down from a military invasion and accepted a negotiated settlement because he estimated that the risk of a more widespread continental war had become too great. There were also doubts about the nation's readiness for war. A government agency reported that:

1   ... There is no enthusiasm for military entanglements on account of the Sudeten German question. The uncertainty of the political situation is making the population depressed. Nobody wants to contemplate a war with England and France. The education of the whole nation in the tasks
5   required by a total war with all its burdens of various kinds is by no means adequate.

    The mood is in many cases depressed, mainly on account of the serious concern that sooner or later a war would put an end to the economic boom and would end in disaster for Germany.
10   In view of the diplomatic situation and the prospects for war which are often discussed without inhibition the mood can generally be described as depressed, serious and worried; there is a 'general war psychosis'.

The effects of the Munich Agreement were many and complex. For Germany there were considerable economic and strategic advantages. The Sudetenland was rich in natural deposits of coal, copper and lignite (brown coal); and it was also a strong manufacturing centre for textiles, chemicals and machine tools. All these assets now passed to Germany. Moreover, within the mountains of the Sudetenland, Czechoslovakia had constructed its frontier defences. They too were simply taken over by Germany, thus removing any real defensive capability from the Czech state.

The crisis also had profound implications for European diplomacy and the continental balance of power, since with hindsight it is clear that Hitler was now prepared to pursue a policy of war, although he wanted to fight any conflict on his terms. His ultimate objective was

still the creation of *Lebensraum* at the expense of the USSR, but hopefully this could be facilitated by Britain's appeasement policy developing into a more general acceptance of Germany's dominant position
in central and eastern Europe. As for the USSR, its exclusion from the
decision-making process at Munich was a clear sign of the failure of
the anti-fascist coalition which Stalin had tried to create under the
banner of the 'Popular Front'. Consequently, in the wake of the
Sudeten crisis, Soviet foreign policy began to realign itself towards the
possibility of some sort of understanding with Nazi Germany which
would be aimed at preserving its own national security.

The last few months of peace witnessed frenzied diplomatic
activity. In March 1939 Germany had used diplomatic and military
threats to secure the self-dissolution of the Czech state (the provinces
of Bohemia and Moravia were annexed to Germany and Slovakia
became a German protectorate). Yet, although the Western democracies did not respond militarily to this overturning of the Munich
Agreement, the Anglo-French guarantee of Poland's independence
two weeks later clearly threw doubt on Hitler's hopes of a free hand
in eastern Europe. Some historians have pointed to the various military orders given at this time for the establishment of long-range
bomber squadrons and the construction of a large navy as symbolic of
Hitler's 'internationalist' ambitions and his preparedness to take on
Britain. This may well be the correct analysis of the long-term intention, but in the short term Hitler most definitely did not want a war
with Britain and France.

c) Poland

How could he avoid such a conflict while pursuing his claims against
Poland? In May 1939 he did manage to secure an alliance by the Pact
of Steel with Italy, but this was of limited military significance. It was
the hope of neutralising Britain and France which drove Hitler into
the arms of Stalin. Anglo-French negotiations with the USSR had
made limited progress and Stalin was becoming increasingly convinced that the Western democracies had no real sympathy for Soviet
security concerns. This created a suitable atmosphere in which trade
talks between Germany and the USSR could be re-established in July.
Only a month later, a ten-year Nazi–Soviet Non-Aggression Pact was
signed with additional secret clauses allowing for the division of
eastern Europe into spheres of influence for the two powers.

Hitler was now confident that Western military intervention would
not follow a German invasion of Poland. Even while the negotiations
were still taking place, Hitler told an assembly of senior Army
commanders that there were no grounds for diplomatic or military
doubts.

| ... The enemy had another hope, that Russia would become our enemy
  after the conquest of Poland. The enemy did not reckon with my great

strength of purpose. Our enemies are little worms. I saw them in
Munich ...

5   I shall give a propagandist reason for starting the war, no matter
whether it is plausible or not. The victor will not be asked afterwards
whether he told the truth or not. When starting and waging war it is
not right that matters, but victory ...

    Close your hearts to pity. Act brutally. Eighty million people must
10 obtain what is their right. Their existence must be made secure. The
strongest man is right.

Germany attacked her eastern neighbour on 1 September 1939 as
planned. However, Britain and France stood by their guarantee to
Poland, and two days later they declared war on Germany. Germany
had become embroiled in a major continental conflict which involved
military commitments on both its eastern and western fronts.

4 The Outbreak of War

> **KEY ISSUE** Why did the German invasion of Poland result in a
> continental war in 1939?

By the end of 3 September 1939 Germany was at war not only with
Poland, but also with Britain and France. Ironically, neither of these
two countries, despite the popular backing for the declaration of war,
had any real desire to take the military initiative against Germany, as
was shown by the months of military inactivity which followed. So,
how and why did Germany find itself in this unwanted situation?

    It is hard to escape the conclusion that the fundamental cause lies
with Hitler's grandiose foreign and racial policy. His desire for continental hegemony and the creation of *Lebensraum* at the expense of
the USSR could only realistically be achieved (as he knew very well)
by military force. In this sense the outbreak of some kind of war was
implicit as long as Hitler continued to direct German foreign policy,
simply because he wished to overturn the existing *status quo* within
Europe (and perhaps beyond). This was clearly not acceptable to
many other European countries. However, in 1939 Germany was
neither economically nor militarily prepared for a major continental
war. Hitler only expected to fight a small-scale localised war against
Poland, which would help to bolster Germany for the greater conflict
to come. He was convinced (mainly as a result of advice from
Ribbentrop) that the Western democracies would not intervene, but
in this analysis he was shown to be wrong. Above all, Hitler failed to
appreciate Britain's position. From the outset he had desired an
alliance with Britain and, although this was clearly not a possibility
by 1937, he continued to believe that under pressure some sort of
reciprocal understanding was at least feasible. Undoubtedly,

Chamberlain's own hostility to the USSR, combined with his readiness to pursue the policy of appeasement, contributed to Hitler's misapprehension. However, one of the traditional tenets of British foreign policy had long been to prevent one power dominating the continent of Europe. The annexation of Bohemia and Moravia convinced many in Britain that Germany under Hitler could no longer be trusted. Thus, despite Chamberlain's personal prevarications, attitudes in Britain towards Germany changed fundamentally and this made another 'Munich' in 1939 an impossibility. Britain and France guaranteed the independence of Poland in the hope of restraining Hitler and, although they were in a weak diplomatic position after the Nazi–Soviet Pact, they continued to stand by that guarantee. Consequently, when German forces did attack Poland, Britain and France – against the expectations of Hitler – actually did declare war on Germany.

5 Germany at War, 1939–45

> **KEY ISSUE** What were the main phases of World War Two?

Although Germany found itself committed to a major war in the autumn of 1939, which Hitler was not expecting to wage until the mid-1940s, it would be wrong to believe that Germany was militarily destined to fail from the start. The string of victories from September 1939 to November 1941 bear witness to the formidable military power exerted by the Nazi war-machine and suggest that Germany did not have to go down the road to total collapse. The fact that it did not do this, so that by early 1943 Germany was facing certain defeat, has to be explained and not merely assumed, as it is tempting to do with all the advantages of hindsight. Germany's eventual defeat was in no sense inevitable at the outset of the war.

a) Initial Victories, 1939–41

Poland's crushing defeat within a few weeks, endured without help from Britain or France, made available valuable raw materials and labour to supplement the aid already being received from the USSR under the terms of the Nazi–Soviet Pact. Hitler was, therefore, keen to maintain the military momentum and planned for an invasion of France to take place as early as November 1939. The German attack was postponed several times, mainly because of the luke-warm attitude of senior Army generals towards such an operation. It did not finally take place until May 1940, thus prolonging the Anglo-French 'Phoney War' for eight months. Hitler's thinking seems to have revolved around the idea of neutralising the Western democracies before turning east again. To that end Germany needed 'to destroy France' and to reduce Britain to compliance with German aspirations on the continent. In this way it was hoped to force Britain, under the pressure of military circumstances, into an accommodation with Germany.

The German defeat of the Low Countries and France in six weeks was a dramatic triumph for both the armed forces and Hitler. Diffident generals could hardly fail to be impressed by the Führer's military and political handling of events. German popular opinion was relieved and exultant. Hitler ruled not only in Berlin but also in Paris, Oslo, Vienna, Prague and Warsaw, while the Third Reich was bordered by the three 'friendly' powers of Spain, Italy and the USSR. It was assumed by many that the war was as good as over.

If common sense and a healthy self-interest had prevailed, Britain would have settled with Germany. But Churchill refused even to countenance negotiations. The implications of this stubbornness for Germany were clear-cut: Germany needed to secure air superiority, to invade Britain and to disable her military and strategic potential. Thus, Germany's failure to win the Battle of Britain in the autumn of 1940 was significant. But even more so was Hitler's personal decision to switch the military focus, and to start preparing for the invasion of the USSR even before Britain had been neutralised. On 18 December 1940 Hitler issued Directive No. 21 for 'Operation Barbarossa', stating that 'The German armed forces must be prepared to crush Soviet Russia in a quick campaign even before the end of the war against England'. This decision can only be explained by Hitler's belief that *Blitzkrieg* tactics could also succeed in bringing a quick victory against the USSR, as they had against Poland, France and many others.

The invasion of the Soviet Union eventually took place in June 1941, having been delayed by the need to secure Germany's southern flank in the Balkans, where Yugoslavia and Greece (the latter following a failed Italian invasion) had sided with Britain. At first all went well. Vast tracts of territory were occupied and thousands of prisoners were taken. Yet the Russians never lost the will to carry on fighting, and by December 1941 differences over military objectives between Hitler and his generals, Anglo-American aid and the snows of Russia had combined to halt the German advance. Hitler's gamble to break the USSR by launching a *Blitzkrieg* invasion had failed and Germany was now committed to the prospect of a long war on two fronts.

b) The Turning of the Tide, December 1941–January 1943

December 1941 was a turning-point in another sense too, for the Japanese attack on the USA's naval base at Pearl Harbor 'globalised' the conflict. Although he was not obliged to do so, Hitler aligned Germany with Japan and declared war on the USA. This move was perhaps prompted by the USA involvement in the Battle of the

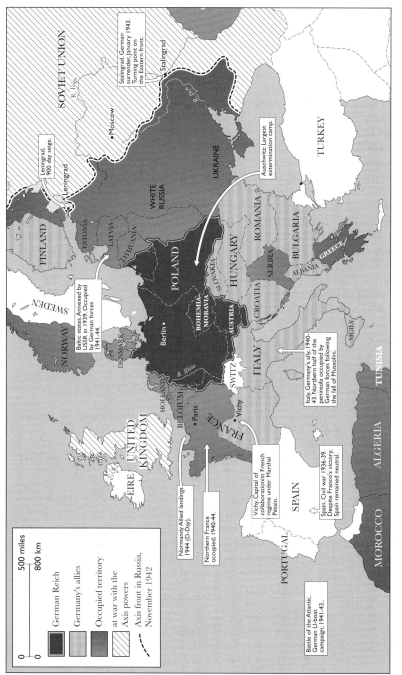

Map of Europe showing Nazi Germany at its height, 1942.

Stalingrad. German surrender, January 1943. Turning point on the Eastern front.

Auschwitz: Largest extermination camp.

Leningrad, 900 day seige.

Baltic states. Annexed by USSR in 1939. Occupied by German forces 1941–44.

Italy. Germany's ally, 1940–43. Northern half of the peninsula occupied by German forces following the fall of Mussolini.

Vichy. Capital of collaborationist French regime under Marshal Pétain.

Normandy Allied landings 1944 (D-Day).

Northern France occupied, 1940–44.

Spain. Civil war 1936–39. Despite Franco's victory, Spain remained neutral.

Battle of the Atlantic. German U-boat campaign, 1941–43.

SOVIET UNION
R. Volga
Stalingrad
Moscow
TURKEY
FINLAND
Leningrad
ESTONIA
LATVIA
LITHUANIA
WHITE RUSSIA
UKRAINE
ROMANIA
BULGARIA
GREECE
ALBANIA
SERBIA
HUNGARY
SLOVAKIA
POLAND
CROATIA
BOHEMIA MORAVIA
AUSTRIA
SWITZ.
ITALY
SICILY
TUNISIA
ALGERIA
MOROCCO
PORTUGAL
SPAIN
FRANCE
Vichy
Paris
R. Rhine
HOLLAND
BELGIUM
Berlin
DENMARK
SWEDEN
NORWAY
UNITED KINGDOM
EIRE

500 miles
800 km

German Reich
Germany's allies
Occupied territory
at war with the Axis powers
Axis front in Russia, November 1942

Atlantic even before Pearl Harbor. However, it did not fit easily with Germany's existing strategy and above all it turned the industrial capacity of the world's greatest power against his own country. It is tempting therefore to suggest that by the end of 1941 Hitler had lost the military and diplomatic grasp which had previously allowed him to shape international developments. Events were now very much running out of the Führer's control. He was beginning to respond to circumstances and to make strategic judgements which were largely shaped by his own capacity for self-delusion and by his own warped view of the world, rather than by any rational assessment of situations.

Although with hindsight it appears that the decisions made by Hitler in December 1941 were indeed the vital turning-point for German fortunes in the war, this was certainly not apparent at the time. Throughout 1942 German forces pushed deep into the Caucasian oilfields with the objective of capturing Stalingrad, while the Afrika Korps drove the British back across North Africa into Egypt. It was the failure of these two offensives which enabled contemporaries to see the winter of 1942–3 as 'the turning of the tide': the British victory at El Alamein (November 1942) eventually led to the ejection of German forces from North Africa; and the encirclement and surrender of 300,000 troops at Stalingrad marked the beginning of the Soviet counter-offensive. The implications of the situation were difficult to hide from the German public:

1 How different the atmosphere is from that of the first war year when
   at the slightest provocation red Nazi flags were flown, drums were
   beaten on the radio announcing victory. Since the defeat at Stalingrad
   and the realisation of total war, all is grey and still and on 14 August
5 [1943] Goebbels declared total war to all at home. Everyone was called
   up, even women up to 50 years old, and mere boys had to do anti-
   aircraft duties.

c) Defeat

From 1943 Germany's strategy was essentially defensive. Hitler was determined to protect 'Fortress Europe' from Allied invasion, but his strategic and political thinking was losing touch with reality. Increasingly it was shaped solely by belief in German invincibility and his own ideological prejudices about race and communism. For, in spite of all the military difficulties, the creation of the new racial order continued – there was no postponement of the programme to exterminate the Jews. Hitler deluded himself into thinking that the alliance of the USSR and the Western Allies could not last and that this would then allow Germany to play off one against the other. However, Allied military co-ordination continued to work reasonably well. By the end of 1943 Anglo-American forces had linked up in Africa and had then established a hold on southern Italy, while Soviet forces, in the wake of the great tank victory at Kursk, had reconquered much of the Ukraine. The war had also begun to have an impact on Germany itself. The massive bombing raids wreaked destruction and dislocation, although their exact strategic value has been questioned over the years. It was becoming clear the war could not be won and that Germany faced total devastation unless the Allied demand for 'unconditional surrender' was conceded. Such realities prompted the attempted assassination of Hitler (see page 144) in July 1944. Its failure meant that the war would have to be fought to the bitter end. Thus, strong German resistance forced the Western Allies to fight extremely hard in order to break out of the beach-head established in Normandy in 1944, whilst in the east the Soviet advance ground remorselessly through eastern Europe in the face of desperate defensive measures. Yet, a blind optimism still prevailed in the minds of some, as Albert Speer, the Minister for Armaments and a close friend of Hitler, later explained.

1   In Westphalia a flat tyre forced us to stop. Unrecognised in the twilight I stood in a farm-yard talking to farmers. To my surprise, the faith in Hitler which had been hammered into their minds all these last years was still strong. Hitler could never lose the war, they declared. 'The
5   Führer is still holding something in reserve that he'll play at the last moment. Then the turning-point will come. It's only a trap, he's letting the enemy come so far into our country.'

It was not until April 1945, when Soviet soldiers had advanced to within a mile of the Chancellery in Berlin, that Hitler committed suicide. Only then was the German nation freed from the Führer's grip and only then could the war end.

6 Conclusion

> **KEY ISSUES** Was Nazi foreign policy fundamentally different from that of Weimar and the Kaiser? Did Germany have to lose the Second World War?

By May 1945 Germany lay in ruins. Nazi foreign policy had reached its destructive and nihilistic conclusion. Its ambitions had been grandiose: to establish a 'greater Germany', which went well beyond the Bismarckian legacy of 1871; to destroy Bolshevik Russia; and to create a new (world?) order based on the concept of Aryan racial supremacy. Moreover, the means to these ends had also involved the acceptance of violence and bloodshed on a massive scale. Yet, it would be incorrect to suggest that German foreign policy had undergone a complete about-turn in 1933. Expansionism clearly stands out as a thread of continuity in German history from the time of the

Kaiserreich onwards. The unexpected failure of Germany to achieve its ambitions in the First World War left a legacy of unrequited aspirations at many levels of German society, which were strengthened by the *Diktat* of Versailles. All Weimar governments were committed to fundamental revision of the Versailles treaty, whilst throughout the 1920s powerful voices in the armed forces continued to advance more radical proposals to restore Germany's continental position.

The development of Nazi foreign policy must, therefore, be viewed in the light of such traditions and circumstances. Hitler advanced ideas sufficiently similar to those of the conservative elites in the Army, foreign ministry and big business for them to gain general acceptance among the established ruling circles in Germany. However, this is not to suggest that Hitler was a mere 'agent' of other social forces. Nor does it imply that there was a clear-cut consensus about the direction of German foreign policy in Party and state. The fact that alternative points of view and strategies continued to exist reflects the rather confused structure of government in the Third Reich. Nevertheless, it is clear that in spite of all the political pressures and demands, the ultimate direction taken by Nazi foreign policy was a reflection of Hitler's personal ideological framework and strategy. In that sense it remains valid to speak of Hitler's foreign policy and Hitler's war.

That Hitler failed in his ambitions can be explained on a superficial level by his strategic bungling. Hitler had always believed (shaped largely by his own personal experiences as a soldier) that a war on two fronts had to be avoided. To this end he needed an alliance with Britain – or at least its benevolent neutrality – so that he could launch an unrestrained attack in the east. Consequently, when Germany failed to secure either British neutrality or a British surrender in 1940–1, before attacking the USSR, the long-term cause of defeat was laid. Germany had become engaged in a conflict for which it was not fully prepared. Moreover, as has been seen in chapter 4, at the start of the war Germany did not exploit the available resources and manpower effectively. The alliance with Mussolini's Italy was no substitute. Indeed, Italian military weakness in the Balkans and North Africa proved costly, since it diverted German forces away from the main European fronts. Yet, Hitler was driven on obsessively to launch the ideological crusade against the USSR. The failure to defeat the Soviet Union before the onset of winter, combined with the entry of the USA, now tipped the balance. Britain was still free to act as a launch-pad for a western front and in the meantime could strike into the heart of Germany by means of aerial bombing. The USSR could maintain the eastern front by relying on its geography and huge manpower. Above all, however, the resources and industrial capacity of the world's two industrial giants were now directed towards the military defeat of Germany.

Such an interpretation might give the impression that historical explanation can be a relatively straightforward exercise. It seems so logical and clear-cut. However, before accepting such a mechanical view of Germany's defeat in the Second World War, it should be borne in mind that even in 1942 Germany came very close indeed to capturing Stalingrad and to defeating Britain in Egypt. Such successes would have changed the course of the war and the final outcome might have been rather different.

References

1 For the 'globalist' view see the works of K. Hildebrand and A. Hillgrüber. For the continentalist view see the works of E. Jäckel.
2 M. Broszat. Quoted in Kershaw, *The Nazi Dictatorship* (Edward Arnold, 3rd ed. 1993) p. 112
3 T. Mason, 'Some Origins of the Second World War' in E.M. Robertson (ed.) *The Origins of the Second World War* (Macmillan, 1971)
4 W.H. Shirer, *The Rise and Fall of the Third Reich* (Pan, 1964) p. 363
5 Ibid. p. 380
6 A.J.P. Taylor, *The Origins of the Second World War* (Hamish Hamilton, 1961) p. 132

Summary diagram
The Rise and Fall of the Third Reich

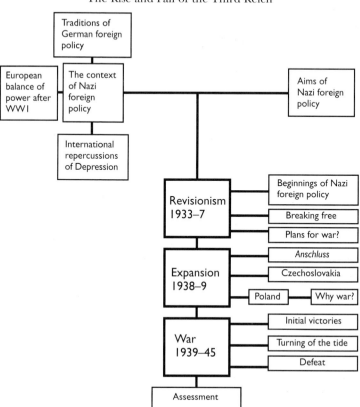

Working on Chapter 7

It is vital to remember that this chapter can serve only as a starting-point for your study of this topic. You will only be able to understand and appreciate the finer points of the debate if you have gained a broader perspective by i) finding out about the development of German foreign policy before 1933; and ii) considering German foreign policy in the broader context of international relations between 1918 and 1945. Those of you following outline courses will probably have done some work on the first issue. If so, now might be a good time to refresh your memory about what you have studied previously. Some of you will also have started to build up a picture of the second issue when studying the history of other states. Again, now would be a good time to look back at some of the notes you made then.

Following the reading of this chapter, there are two important tasks to carry out:

1   Construct two chronological tables – one for the period 1933–9 and one for the period 1939–45. In each case divide your sheet of paper into three columns with the following headings:
    a) Major domestic events in Germany
    b) Initiatives in German foreign policy
    c) International developments
2   You need to begin to grapple with some of the important issues raised about German foreign policy. Therefore, you should try to write summarising answers to the following questions:
    a) What exactly were the foreign policy objectives of Hitler?
    b) To what extent did Hitler's methods of handling foreign policy change over time?
    c) Why is it dangerous to differentiate between the Third Reich's domestic policy (especially in the economic arena) and its foreign policy? (see also chapter 4)
    d) Why did war break out in September 1939?
    e) Why did Germany suffer such a cataclysmic defeat in the war?

Answering source-based questions on Chapter 7

1. Hitler's Attitude to War
Study the two extracts from Hitler's speeches on pages 122 and 129–30. Answer the following questions:

a) Explain 'I saw them in Munich' (page 130 lines 3–4). (*1 mark*)
b) Comment on the contrast in tone and language between the two extracts. (*3 marks*)
c) How do you explain the differences between the two extracts? (*4 marks*)

d) Explain in your own words how Hitler assessed Allied diplomacy in 1939. Do you think that his assessment was accurate? (*5 marks*)

e) 'The war of 1939 was far from premeditated. It was an avoidable mistake.' How far do these sources and other evidence known to you support this assertion? (*7 marks*)

2. Public Opinion and Foreign Affairs, 1936–9

Study the three extracts commenting on public opinion on pages 123, 126 and 128. Answer the following questions.

a) Explain **i)** 'the Sudeten German question' (page 128 line 2), and **ii)** 'the junking of Versailles' (page 123 line 6). (*4 marks*)

b) How do the authors of the first two extracts explain the high percentage of votes cast in favour of Hitler's regime in the plebiscites? Refer to similarities and differences. (*6 marks*)

c) How do you explain the conclusion reached by the third extract? (*4 marks*)

d) What problems do these extracts highlight about the assessment of public opinion under a dictatorship? (*6 marks*)

3. Popular Attitudes to the War

Study the two extracts on pages 134 and 135. Answer the following questions.

a) Explain **i)** 'total war' (page 134 line 4), and **ii)** 'defeat at Stalingrad' (page 134 line 3). (*2 marks*)

b) What might be the reasons for the contrast in public expectation described in the two extracts? (*4 marks*)

c) Assess the reliability of these two sources as evidence of popular attitudes towards the war. (*4 marks*)

You will undoubtedly be aware of the need to evaluate the reliability of documents in all source-based questions. Hitler's two speeches in question 1 are a very good example of how you need to get behind what has been said. The content and the tone are markedly different. As a starting-point you should always consider the time and context and the intended audience. So what is the international context in May 1935? And to whom is Hitler directing his words in the first document? What is he trying to achieve by such comments? In contrast in the second document Hitler was speaking on 22 August 1939 (a very specific and a very significant date). How has the international context changed? Why can he now speak in such bellicose terms? What does he want to achieve by this speech? Now look at question 3 on Popular Attitudes to the War. The first extract is from a private diary written by an ordinary citizen in 1943 and the second is from a book written in 1970 by Albert Speer after he was released from prison by the Allies. How do these facts help you to make an evaluation of reliability? What is the general problem with any assessment of public opinion in the past?

The German Resistance: Opposition in the Third Reich

8

POINTS TO CONSIDER

This chapter considers the issue of *German* 'resistance', in its broadest sense, to the Third Reich. To appreciate some of the subtleties involved in this historical minefield will require careful thought and reading over a period of time. So your aim as you read this chapter for the first time should simply be to understand the different ways in which 'resistance' has been interpreted and to recognise how acts of resistance took a wide variety of forms.

KEY DATES

1934	May	Establishment of Confessional Church to resist Nazi control of the Protestant Church.
1935		Mass arrests by Gestapo of socialists and communists.
1938		Planned *putsch* by General Beck if war resulted from Czech crisis.
1941	Aug	Bishop Galen's sermon against euthanasia.
1942–3		White Rose student group; distribution of anti-Nazi leaflets.
1944	July	Stauffenberg Bomb Plot on 20 July failed to overthrow regime.
	Nov	Execution of 12 Edelweiss Pirates in Cologne.

1 Resistance: the Problems of Definition and Research

> **KEY ISSUE** Why has the term 'resistance' caused so many difficulties for students and historians of Nazi Germany?

It has already been suggested that the images projected and fostered by Nazism of a united *Volksgemeinschaft* in reality fell short of the intended aims and aspirations of the regime. However, any attempt to gauge the extent of 'resistance' (and, by implication, collaboration) within the Third Reich is a historical problem fraught with difficulties. The student must therefore approach this particular aspect of Nazi Germany in the knowledge that any conclusions will inevitably be tentative. In particular, it should be borne in mind that any conclusions reached are deeply affected by approaching the research into the subject in alternative ways or by applying different criteria in one's assessment.

The very word 'resistance' is a problem in itself. We may be able to agree that the use of the term as applied to para-military movements like the French *maquis*, who were fighting an alien occupying force, is not really appropriate but what exactly constituted 'resistance' inside Nazi Germany? For some, it can only be interpreted as the deliberate attempt to subvert and to bring an end to the regime. At the other end of the scale, it has been viewed as any behaviour which falls short of wholesale support for the regime. Such widely differing definitions not only create clear gulfs between historians, but each one also generates further serious implications. By accepting the narrow definition one is drawn to the conclusion that there were just a few heroic German resistors, which in turn could lead to the 'charge' that the Third Reich was generally accepted. In this way the historical debate about resistance has profound political and moral overtones that still reverberate in modern-day Germany. By contrast, the broader definition of resistance has inevitably tended to highlight the limits of collaboration and conformity in Nazi Germany. This has been achieved by adopting less traditional research methods, such as oral history, in an attempt to measure more broadly people's feelings, attitudes and behaviour in the Third Reich. Not surprisingly, such a methodology has been criticised by those who see it as trying to water down fundamental active resistance and to exaggerate the importance of more passive behaviour which had little or real effect on the actual power of the regime.

However, whatever definition of resistance is used, it is still vital for the historian to be aware of the particular problems posed by evaluating sources which emanate from the time of the Third Reich. Any attempt to measure the nature and extent of resistance has to take into account the exceptional circumstances. The Third Reich was a regime built upon an apparatus of terror and surveillance. It was almost impossible to make any gesture of opposition to the regime without risk to oneself or one's family. Furthermore, the idea that such an action should be supported by written documentation would have seemed ludicrous. Therefore, trying to ascertain what people at the time really did believe and do (as opposed to what the Nazis wanted them to believe and do) is far from easy. Finally, it must be borne in mind that the Third Reich lasted for over twelve years and the historical situation was far from static. Over the years circumstances changed and, not surprisingly, people's responses were not always uniform or consistent. Many people's attitudes changed over time and support for the regime on one issue could give way to outright opposition on another.

2 Active Resistance

KEY ISSUE Why did all attempts to weaken the Third Reich end in relative failure?

In the twenty or so years after the Second World War numerous studies were published in Germany of what was termed 'active resistance'. In general this was taken to mean organised activities aimed at subverting the regime. Marxist historians from East Germany concentrated almost exclusively on the role of the internal communist opposition and portrayed it as the midwife to Germany's liberation from fascism by the Soviet Union. In West Germany, on the other hand, the thrust of historical writing tended to highlight those elements which had valiantly tried to keep alight the flame of freedom and liberalism. Consequently, the focus of research, though not ignoring the Churches and students, was on the role of the traditional elites and conservatives. Yet, it was difficult to escape from the conclusion that all representatives of 'active resistance' – however gloriously and heroically portrayed – made enormous personal sacrifices without making any real impression on the Nazi stranglehold of power. Why was this?

a) Communists

Although the KPD had a mass membership of 300,000 and it polled 17 per cent of the popular vote in 1932, it felt the full force of Nazi co-ordination and repression from the very start. Over half of its members were interned during the first year of Nazi rule. By 1935 the Gestapo had infiltrated the remnants of the party, which had tried to continue with the distribution of printed material and involvement in minor acts of sabotage. There followed a series of mass trials, though the Communist underground movement was never entirely broken in spite of this onslaught. After 1936 activists were also drawn to fight for the Republicans in the Spanish Civil War, in the belief that such a gesture was a more worthwhile way of resisting fascism. The most famous of its cells was the so-called *Rote Kapelle* (Red Orchestra), a Communist spy network which successfully permeated elements of both the government and military and from 1938 to 1942 transmitted vital information back to Moscow. However, the impact of such activities should not be overstated. The Communists were fatally compromised by the Nazi–Soviet Pact of 1939–41 and even when the USSR and Germany did end up at war with each other they remained isolated from other resistance groups. Active Communist resistance to the Nazi state was limited and in the end it became more geared towards self-preservation, so that it was at least ready for the day when Nazism could be undone and the revolution ushered in by the external might of the Red Army.

b) Students: The White Rose Group

The White Rose student resistance movement is probably the most famous of the youth groups because it went beyond mere nonconformity. It was led by brother and sister Hans and Sophie Scholl. *The White Rose* was the name given to a series of leaflets printed in 1942–3 and distributed initially amongst the students of Munich University but in time to many towns in Central Germany. The content of the leaflets was highly political and openly condemned the moral and spiritual values of the Nazi regime. One of the early leaflets was entitled 'Isn't every decent German today ashamed of his government?'. The group represented a brave gesture of defiance and self-sacrifice for it was only a matter of time before the Gestapo closed in. In February 1943 the six leaders were arrested and swiftly executed.

c) Conservative Elites

It might seem surprising that the most potent active resistance emerged from the ranks of Germany's upper classes, who dominated the civil service and most particularly the officer corps. After all, these were the same conservative nationalists whose lack of support for Weimar democracy had encouraged them to give sympathetic backing to the establishment of Nazi authoritarianism. On the other hand, the Army as an elite institution had never been fully co-ordinated and therefore enjoyed a degree of autonomy from Nazi control. Moreover, the Army with its access to arms had the material capacity for effecting physical resistance, unlike any other institution. For these reasons the development of the conservative resistance coalesced around the Army, though once again it was to fail in its primary objective.

The opposition of the conservative elites emerged slowly. At first, most conservatives could only support and applaud in varying degrees the creation of the Third Reich, its attacks on the left wing, its dismantling of the democratic system and the restoration of authoritarian rule, its vilification of Versailles, and its demands for revision and rearmament. Most significantly, the Army gave its blessing to the Night of the Long Knives and fatally compromised itself with the regime. At first, then, the conservative elites did not recognise – or did not want to recognise – the true radical nature of Nazism, and unwittingly strengthened the regime to such an extent that resistance thereafter became much more difficult.

1938 marked a watershed in the emergence of what became the conservative resistance. Ulrich von Hassell, the ex-ambassador in Rome, and Carl Goerdeler, Mayor of Leipzig and a one-time member of Hitler's early government, both went over to the side of the Nazi opposition at this time. More significantly, Ludwig Beck, formerly Chief of the General Staff, became convinced by the summer of 1938 that Hitler's intention to invade Czechoslovakia could only lead to continental war. Plans were drawn up to stage a *coup* and overtures were also made to the British Foreign Office. As it happened, the Allied appeasement of Hitler at Munich cut the ground from beneath the conspirators and the planned revolt was dropped while Hitler basked in the glory of his diplomatic gains.

Resistance began to re-emerge in the winter of 1942–3. The so-called Kreisau Circle was a wide-ranging group of officers, aristocrats, academics and churchmen who met at the Kreisau estate of Helmut von Moltke. The conferences discussed ideas about plans for a new Germany after Hitler and in August 1943 a programme was drawn up (see page 145). The principles of the Kreisau circle were politically conservative and strongly influenced by Christian values. Indeed, the pacifist element was sufficiently strong for the group to oppose a *coup* against Hitler. Nevertheless, some individual members were supporters of what became the most far-reaching act of resistance to Hitler's Germany – the Bomb Plot of 1944. A number of the civilian resistance figures made contact with dissident Army officers, such as Beck and Tresckow, in order to plan the assassination of Hitler and the creation of a provisional government. Eventually, the lead was taken by Colonel von Stauffenberg who placed a bomb in Hitler's briefing room at his headquarters in East Prussia on 20 July 1944. The bomb exploded, but Hitler sustained only minor injuries, and in the confused aftermath the generals in Berlin fatally hesitated, thus enabling a group of loyal soldiers to arrest the conspirators and re-establish order.

The conservative elites proved incapable of fundamentally weakening the Nazi regime and in that sense they failed. They only recognised the need to resist once the regime was well-established and after that the planning and organisation of effective action was always fraught with difficulties. Their long-term political aims lacked clarity and practical plans were always inhibited by the environment of suspicion and uncertainty which pervaded a police state. In the end the bad luck and confusion of the Bomb Plot of 20 July reflected those difficulties.

3 Passive Resistance

> **KEY ISSUES** What is meant by 'passive resistance'? In what ways did anti-Nazi dissent reveal itself?

It is apparent from the above analysis that active resistance was limited in scope and achieved very little. It is therefore perhaps tempting to assume that this reflected an implicit acceptance of the Third Reich by the German population. As one historian has put it, this was 'resistance without the people'.[1] Such a view would be simplistic and has been questioned by a generation of historians since the 1970s who have refined the concept of resistance and adopted new research techniques in order to examine more closely popular attitudes and

The Aims of the Resistance

A. ... It seems to me that a hereditary monarchy is the form of state for our people. Our fickle, unpolitical people needs ballast in the ship of state. The monarch shall not govern but shall watch over the constitution and represent the state. The House of Hohenzollern and the House of Wittelsbach could provide worthy monarchs ... If it is not possible to put a monarchy in the saddle, then things have to remain with a *Reichspresident* who must be eligible for unlimited re-election and who after his election for the third time can also be elected for life.
(C. Goerdeler. Part of a draft constitution drawn up in September 1944 whilst in prison following the Bomb Plot)

B. ... The government of the German Reich sees in Christianity the basis for the ethical and religious revival of our people, for the conquest of hatred and lies, for the creation anew of the European community of people ...
1. Justice, fallen and trampled, must be restored, and must be made supreme over all orders of human life. This justice, under the protection of conscientious, independent judges who are free from fear of men, will be the basis for the future moulding of peace.
2. Freedom of faith and conscience is guaranteed.
3. The right of work and property stands under public protection without regard to race, nationality or creed.
4. The basic unit of peaceful community life is the family.
5. Work must be arranged in such a way that it fosters rather than stunts the enjoyment of personal responsibility.
6. The personal political responsibility of everyone requires his co-determining participation in the self-administration of the small communities.
(Programme of the Kreisau Circle drafted in 1943)

C. We desire a new order that makes all Germans the bearers of the state and guarantees to them law and justice; but we despise the lie of equality and bow before the ranks created by nature. We desire a people that, rooted in the soil of their homeland, remains close to the natural forces, that finds happiness and satisfaction in working within its given spheres ... We desire leaders who, drawn from all ranks of the people, and linked with the divine powers, rise above all by their discipline and sacrifice.
(Draft of an oath drawn up by Stauffenberg shortly before his death)

D. The assassination must take place, whatever the cost. Even if it should fail, the attempt to seize power in Berlin must take place. The practical consequences are immaterial. The German resistance must prove to the world and to posterity that it dares to take the decisive step.
(Statement by Tresckow to Stauffenberg in June 1944)

beliefs. This new approach was part of a trend towards *Alltagsgeschichte* (the history of everyday life) which quite deliberately shifted the focus of historical analysis on to the grass-roots of society. This was most obviously epitomised by the so-called Bavaria Project led by Mommsen and Huttenberger, which eventually produced in the ten years 1973–83 six volumes on *Resistance and Persecution in Bavaria, 1933–45*. Their starting-point was to reinterpret the concept of resistance on the premise that in a totalitarian dictatorship, as opposed to a pluralistic democracy, any action which questioned the state's totalitarian claims qualified as a kind of resistance. Thus resistance became redefined as 'every form of active or passive behaviour which allows recognition of the rejection of the National Socialist regime or a partial area of National Socialist ideology and was bound up with certain risks'.[2] This much broader definition of resistance therefore held that simply the failure to conform to Nazi expectations amounted to an act of resistance, albeit of a passive kind. Rather confusingly this idea in German has been termed *Resistenz*. However, its meaning in English is closest to the idea of resistance in physics, where the flow of current is reduced. In the context of the Third Reich this broad and variable view of what could be deemed resistance not surprisingly has generated considerable controversy. It has also in effect opened up a whole new debate about public opinion under the Nazis, so that the traditional view of active resistance has to be viewed alongside the more passive resistance of dissent and nonconformity and also by extension alongside the attitudes of consent and collaboration.

What did passive resistance amount to? Clearly it fell a long way short of the heroic gestures of Stauffenberg or the brave actions of the Scholls and at first sight its manifestations might seem incredibly mundane. However, it is important to bear in mind the context. Nazi Germany was a society where the refusal to give the 'Heil Hitler' salute could be deemed an act of dissent and held against someone. The same could be said of anyone telling anti-Nazi jokes or refusing to hang out a Nazi flag. It demanded from its people a degree of social conformity which included the rejection of jazz and swing music as decadent. In the end it was even designated a criminal offence in Nazi Germany to listen to foreign radio broadcasts or to fraternise with foreign workers.

a) Youth

It is all too easy to be lulled into believing that German youth was a relatively secure bastion of Nazi conformity when one looks at the newsreel pictures of the Hitler Youth with its images of camaraderie and youthful exuberance for the cause. However, much recent research suggests that sizeable pockets of the adolescent population had not been won over by 1939 and that, during the war, alienation and dissent increased quite markedly. The regime even established a special youth section of the secret police and a youth concentration camp was set up at Neuwied. A number of youth groups developed which quite deliberately exhibited a code of behaviour at odds with the expected social values. 'Swing Youth' was one such craze among mainly middle-class youngsters who took up the music and imagery associated with the dance-bands of Britain and the USA. The *Edelweiss Piraten* (the edelweiss is a white alpine flower which served as a symbol of opposition) was a general name given to a host of working-class youths who formed gangs such as the 'Roving Dudes' and 'Navajos'. Their members had been alienated by the military emphasis and discipline of the Hitler Youth. They met up and organised their own hikes and camps which then came into conflict with the official ones. In several instances, 'Pirates' became involved in more active resistance, most famously at Cologne in 1944 when twelve of them were publicly hanged because of their attacks on military targets and the assassination of a Gestapo officer.

b) Christians

It has already been suggested in chapter 5 (see pages 78–81) that the Nazis only achieved limited success in their religious policy. However, it could also be maintained that both the Catholic and Protestant Churches failed because of their inability to provide effective resistance to Nazism. Neither of the Christian Churches were 'co-ordinated' and therefore both enjoyed a measure of independence which could have provided the focus for active resistance. Instead, they preferred as institutions to adopt a pragmatic policy towards the Nazis. They stood up for their own practices and traditions, but generally refrained from wholesale denunciations of the regime. The reason for this lies in the conservatism of both Churches. They distrusted the politics of the left which seemed to threaten the existing order of society and which in its most extreme form, atheistic communism, rejected the existence of religion itself. Equally though, there was a nationalist sympathy for Nazism, especially after the problems of 1918–33. It was all too easy to believe that Hitler's 'national renewal' was simply a return to the halcyon days before 1914. This was particularly true of the Protestant Church, which since the time of Luther had been closely aligned to the state apparatus. Finally, both Churches rightly feared the power of the Nazi state, and they believed that any gestures of heroic resistance were more than likely to have bloody consequences. In such a situation, concentration on pastoral and spiritual comfort was perhaps the most practical and realistic policy for the Churches.

Effective Christian resistance, therefore, remained essentially the preserve of individual churchmen who put their own freedom and lives at risk in order to uphold their beliefs or to give pastoral assistance. Most famous were: Dietrich Bonhoeffer, whose opposition brought him into direct contact with elements of the conservative resistance; Martin Niemöller, the founder of the Confessional Church, who languished in a concentration camp from 1937; and Bishop Galen of Münster, whose outspoken sermon attacking Nazi euthanasia policy in 1941 proved so powerful that the authorities recoiled from arresting him and actually stopped the programme. Such heroic examples were by no means exceptional and hundreds of priests and pastors were to die in the camps for their refusal to co-operate with the regime. Their sacrifice is therefore eloquent testimony to the limits of conformity. But it also bears witness to the fact that such courageous resistance was rarely able to restrain the regime.

c) Workers

Although the vast majority of workers did not engage in the active resistance encouraged by the Communist cells, the working class had a clearly established sub-culture in the trade unions, working men's clubs and SPD/KPD party organisations which provided an identity and association at odds with Nazism. This alternative 'identity' did enable opposition to survive and occasionally to express itself. There were a number of strikes in the years 1935–6 and also, not surprisingly, in the last few months of the regime. However, industrial action proved to be ineffective and, on balance, more often than not was motivated by economic discontent at working conditions or price rises rather than political aims. Moreover, reports of low morale and poor work discipline, whilst not suggesting universal enthusiastic endorsement of the regime, were not perceived as sufficiently threatening to change the fundamental direction of the regime.

4 Models of Resistance

KEY ISSUE In what ways have historians tried to differentiate more clearly between different kinds of resistance?

The previous two sections have drawn attention to various examples of resistance using the somewhat simplistic distinction between active and passive behaviour. Hopefully, it has shown that, unless one adheres rigidly to a very narrow definition of resistance (as some historians still do), the broader view of resistance has prompted a more general debate about the whole question of public opinion in Nazi Germany. However, this has made the task of trying to reach conclusions on the success and/or impact of resistance particularly difficult. One historian somewhat cynically notes that there has been a 'tendency to expand the concept of resistance until it covers anything short

A. Botz's pyramid

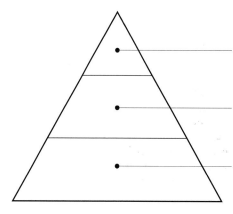

POLITICAL RESISTANCE
eg conspiracy, distribution of
oppositional information, sabotage

SOCIAL PROTEST
eg listening to foreign broadcasts,
sermons critical of anti-church policy

DEVIANT BEHAVIOUR
eg workers' absenteeism

B. Kershaw's concentric circles

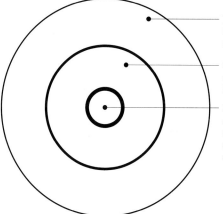

DISSENT
Oppositional feeling which did
not result in action

OPPOSITION
Action with partial and
limited aims

RESISTANCE
Active participation in
organised attempts to work
against the regime with the
aim of undermining it

C. Housden's levels of action

1. Personal mental protection.
2. The deliberate carrying on of traditional community life in the face of Nazi preferences to the contrary.
3. Anti-Nazi discussions with a close circle of friends.
4. Open dissent.
5. Public protest.
6. Concerted conspiracy using low-key means (for example the secret distribution of leaflets) to subvert Nazi policies.
7. Open rebellion against elements of the Hitler state.
8. Revolution against the whole Hitler state.

Models of Resistance.

of positive enthusiasm for the regime'.³ As a result, some historians, in an attempt to give clearer definition to the subtle differences in modes of behaviour, have proposed 'models' of resistance in a manner more akin to the methods of social scientists.

The models shown on page 149 are merely the suggestions of three historians who have tried to categorise resistance. None of them should be seen as providing all the answers to the intellectual problems raised. Indeed, they are probably best viewed as starting-points for discussion and analysis. Once again, a lot clearly depends on the particular meanings applied to specific words. More significantly, there are dangers in the drawing of clear-cut boundary-lines because what emerges from all the research is that any individual's behaviour was rarely clear-cut. More often than not, any one person exhibited a confused mixture of attitudes – variously shaped by religious, financial, moral or personal influences. For example, it was quite feasible for a Catholic priest according to Housden's levels of action to: a) protest publicly over Nazi eugenics or b) deliberately carry on traditional Catholic customs within the community, whilst generally being supportive of Nazi foreign/military policy and perhaps sympathising with the more authoritarian nature of Nazi government. It should also be borne in mind that attitudes were rarely static – circumstances changed dramatically in the twelve years of the Third Reich. Therefore it should be no surprise that that any attempt to make general statements about public opinion must take into account change over time. Indeed, some of the most important figures in the active resistance among the conservative elites had initially supported the Nazi regime enthusiastically.

5 The Extent of Opposition

> **KEY ISSUE** How much opposition was there amongst the German population to the Nazi regime?

The real threat posed by those who opposed the regime was in actual fact fairly limited. Active resistance to undermine the Nazi state could only ever have come from the elites and their disillusion did not crystallise sufficiently until well after they had already helped to establish the Nazi hold on power. It is also clear that the conservative opposition did not enjoy a sufficiently strong and broad base of support at any time. There remains considerable doubt about whether, even if Stauffenberg's bomb had killed Hitler, the plotters would have received the level of support required to bring an immediate end to the Nazi regime. Obviously, the demands of conspiracy inevitably fostered isolation, but in the final analysis the extent of passive resistance was unlikely ever to provide a sufficiently powerful groundswell of support for the likes of Stauffenberg. It was even less likely to inhibit the basic thrust of Nazi policies or threaten the security of the Nazi state. One of Germany's leading historians in this area has written:

> 1 Whatever the perceptible reserve and discontent of the workers, sections of the middle class, and the peasantry, the fact cannot be ignored that the leadership of the Third Reich largely succeeded in producing such a degree of conformity, indeed readiness to collaborate, that its
> 5 plans, especially preparation for war, were not endangered from within.[4]

However, equally it would now seem safe to conclude that the Third Reich fell a long way short of winning the hearts and minds of the German population. The extent of German opposition now revealed in all its forms has shown the limits of Nazi totalitarian aspirations. It could be argued that twelve years was just not a long enough time to achieve the desired level of penetration in German society, but actually the duration of the regime was probably not a vital factor, as the levels of opposition actually increased over time. This was because Nazi radicalism expressed itself in increasingly extreme policies which resulted in an ever wider range of personal economic and moral pressures for all those living in the Third Reich.

Even so, it required, in the words of Kershaw, 'a quantum leap in attitude and behaviour'[5] to cross the boundary from passive to active resistance. After all, the Third Reich was a regime built upon terror and backed up by advanced systems of surveillance and censorship. It was also supported by a propaganda machine which effectively upheld the myth of Hitler's invincibility to the very end. For many, it was perhaps easier to believe the propaganda than to question it. It is all too easy, from the standpoint of our open liberal democracy and with the advantages of hindsight, to dismiss its impact or to sneer at the gullibility of those who were taken in. To have lived in a society where only one point of view was disseminated must have blunted one's powers of judgement. Those individuals who were able to cross the boundary, like the Scholls, must have known that their actions could only ever be a gesture which would end in personal sacrifice and without real effect. Finally, for many people doubts about the regime could be offset by the perceived successes of the regime. Apparent economic recovery and foreign policy triumphs allowed doubts to be pushed to one side or to remain dormant. In the final analysis, very few Germans had the moral courage to make the 'quantum leap' required. Those who did deserve our utmost respect, but one should be wary of morally condemning the many who could not.

References

1   A phrase used by H. Mommsen and quoted in I. Kershaw, *The Nazi Dictatorship* 3rd ed. (London, 1993) p. 150
2   Ibid. p. 158
3   R. Evans quoted in I. Kershaw, op.cit. p. 169
4   P. Huttenberger quoted in Kershaw, op. cit. p. 167
5   Kershaw, op. cit. p. 171

Summary Diagram
Resistance

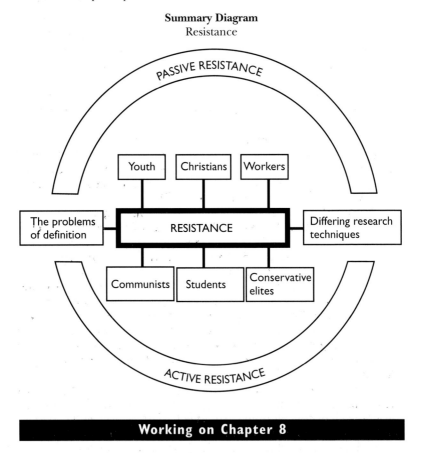

This is quite a difficult chapter to work on. The level of detail is not that great, but the content raises numerous issues of definition and interpretation and your main task must be to try to think through these satisfactorily.

First of all, it would be a good idea to discuss in a small group what exactly the key words mean and what their implications are. Attempt this with the following words: opposition, resistance (passive and active), dissent, non-conformity, conformity, and collaboration. Do your definitions change depending upon the kind of society? Next draw the models of resistance on page 149 but leave enough space to add real examples from sections 2 and 3 of the text. Which of the three models do you find the most satisfactory and why? Afterwards make certain you can answer satisfactorily the questions from the issues boxes in these sections. Finally, read through section 5 again very carefully. Do you agree with the author's claim in the first sentence?

Answering source-based questions on Chapter 8

1. The Aims of the Resistance
Read the boxed extracts on page 145 on 'The Aims of the Resistance'. Answer the following questions:

a) On what grounds does Tresckow justify the assassination attempt? (*3 marks*)
b) Would you agree that the programme of the Kreisau Circle was unrealistic and utopian? (*4 marks*)
c) To what extent do the statements of Goerdeler and Stauffenberg suggest that they were both against Hitler, whilst being unsympathetic to democracy? (*6 marks*)
d) Do you think the statements of Goerdeler and Stauffenberg provide a reliable view of their beliefs? (*5 marks*)
e) To what extent do these documents and other evidence known to you support the assertion that the active resistance to National Socialism was fundamentally divided in its aims? (*7 marks*)

The last question in a series of source-based questions is sometimes a kind of mini-essay (and it can often be worth the most marks). However, it is a mini-essay linked to the sources, in which you have to test an assertion or premise. To this end, it is vital that you look at the given sources and relate them to the question, as well as bringing in other evidence. By 'other evidence' the question means both primary and secondary sources and also your general historical knowledge of the specific topic. Therefore in question 1) e) you could also allude to the leaflets of the White Rose Group, the subversive activities of the Communists and the conspiratorial plans of Ludwig Beck. You could even make the point that on the issue of resistance aims there is only a limited amount of primary evidence – why might this be the case? It is also a good idea to provide a mini-conclusion of 3–4 lines which tries to draw together your analytical comments.

9 The Third Reich and German History

POINTS TO CONSIDER

More than any other chapter in the book this one is intended to form the basis for further thought and discussion. It tries to describe and explain a variety of interpretations of the Third Reich by both contemporaries and historians. As you read it for the first time, try to keep in mind the key issue of how the Third Reich has been thought to fit into the broader context of German history. It would also be a good idea, before you start, to look at the notes you made on chapter 1 to make certain you are aware of the main areas of controversy.

From the outset, the emergence of the Nazi regime presented observers not only with profound political and economic questions but also with serious moral issues to resolve. For example, most left-wing and liberal intellectuals saw Nazism as an essentially evil (and therefore morally reprehensible) movement. This moral dimension has not disappeared with the passage of time, even though Nazism is now a historical issue. Indeed, with the revelations of the full extent of the Nazi horror in 1944–5, the continued reference to war anniversaries in the media and still the occasional story of 'war criminals' and 'war crimes', it is almost impossible not to explain the rise of Nazism without giving consideration to its moral implications. Thus even the seemingly most objective of historical questions are likely to be answered with more than a small amount of subjectivity. Was the Third Reich a natural outgrowth of German history? How crucial was the role of Hitler himself to the Third Reich? To what extent has post-war Germany overcome the Nazi legacy? Such questions have been at the heart of the debate on Nazism. The modern student is therefore already faced with a wide variety of possible answers and historical interpretations, and these continue to be added to as new evidence becomes available and as new generations view events with different perspectives.

1 The Historiography of the Third Reich

> **KEY ISSUE** In what ways have interpretations of Nazism changed over time?

a) Contemporary Views

In the 1930s left-wing analysts faced considerable difficulties in their attempts to explain the rise of Nazism (and by extension of fascism in general), since Marxist dialectics had made no provision for the development of such a movement. Eventually, at the Seventh Congress of the Communist International in 1935, fascism was defined as 'the open terroristic dictatorship of the most reactionary, most chauvinistic and most imperialist elements of finance capital'. And this in fact remained the ideological basis of Marxist scholarship on Nazism until the demise of communism. Stripped of its verbiage, the theory proposes a close connection between Nazism and capitalism. More particularly, it views the Nazis as mere agents for the string-pulling capitalists, who, in order to satisfy their imperialist ambitions and their desire for profits, dominated a powerful political movement so as to suppress the revolutionary workers. According to such a Marxist interpretation, therefore, fascism represented the last stage of capitalism, which would soon collapse because of its own internal contradictions and would thus usher in the age of socialism.

The difficulty with any 'generic' explanation of the rise of European fascism is to substantiate it convincingly with historical detail in particular cases. With Germany in the 1930s the evidence is unconvincing. Contacts did exist between Nazism and big business, and the Nazis did receive financial backing (see page 110) from many major industrialists. However, it is difficult to substantiate the claim that the Nazis were merely the agents in this group. 'The "agent theory" is unable to expose the transmission belts between the monopoly capitalist and their agents.'[1] Moreover, in their attempt to explain fascism in economic terms, Marxist analysts neglected important political aspects. Greater emphasis on the 37 per cent of the population who actually voted for Hitler in 1932 would surely have persuaded the Communist International that National Socialism was something more than a movement of financial capitalists at a time of economic crisis.

However, left-wing arguments were matched by some equally unquestioning views in more conservative circles. When Britain found itself at war with Germany again in 1939 some strong opinions were expressed about the reasons behind the emergence of Hitler's regime. In 1941 Sir Robert Vansittart, Chief Diplomatic Adviser, gave a series of radio broadcasts entitled 'Black Record – Germans Past and Present'. He upheld the view that 'Germany as a whole has always been hostile and unsuited to democracy', and claimed that Hitler's dictatorship had evolved from the authoritarian system of Bismarck and the Kaiser: 'No other race could have managed to idolise such people.'[2]

Vansittart's views can be put down to his long-standing anti-German feelings and to the requirements of war-time propaganda. However, some academic historians of the 1940s also followed a similar line of thought, so that even the renowned A.J.P. Taylor wrote in *The Course of German History* in 1945:

ı It [the Third Reich] was a system founded on terror, unworkable without the secret police and the concentration camp; but it was also a
   system which represented the deepest wishes of the German people. In
   fact it was the only system of government ever created by German
5 initiative ... it rested solely on German force and German impulse; it
   owed nothing to alien forces.[3]

Not surprisingly, such views were not uncommon in those countries
at war with the Third Reich in the early 1940s.

b) Post-War Interpretations

In the years immediately after the Second World War two major lines
of interpretation prevailed. There were those non-German historians
who continued to argue in much the same vein as Vansittart had
done. The culmination of this view was probably reached with the
publication in 1959 of William Shirer's *Rise and Fall of the Third Reich.*
This monumental work, written by an American journalist who had
worked as a correspondent in Germany between 1926 and 1941,
made a profound impact on the general public. In it he explained
how Nazism was 'but a logical continuation of German history'. He
argued that Germany's political evolution, its cultural and intellectual
heritage and the people's national character were all contributory factors in providing German historical development with an inner logic
which led inevitably to the success of Hitler and the creation of the
Third Reich.[4]

Not surprisingly, the implicit anti-German sentiments of historians
from Allied countries were not kindly received in Germany, especially
amongst those intellectuals who had in fact opposed Hitler. As a consequence, there emerged in the post-war decade in West Germany a
school of thought which emphasised the 'moral crisis of European
society'. It was epitomised above all by the writings of G. Ritter who
focused on the European circumstances in which Nazism had
emerged. In his view, it was hard to believe that Germany's great political traditions, such as the power of the Prussian state, or its rich cultural history could have contributed to the emergence of Hitler.
Instead, Ritter emphasised the events and developments since 1914 in
Europe as a whole. It was the shock given to the traditional European
order by the First World War which created the appropriate environment for the emergence of Nazism: the decline in religion and the
traditional standards of morality; a tendency towards corruption and
materialism; above all, it was the emergence of mass democracy at
such a time, which a cynical demagogue like Hitler could exploit for
the satisfaction of his own ends.[5]

The 1960s witnessed the beginnings of a phenomenal growth in
academic literature on the Third Reich. This was partly due to the fact
that the German archives in the hands of the Western Allies were

made available, but it was also a result of the major controversy generated by the publication of a book ironically not even on the subject of Nazi Germany. Fritz Fischer's *Griff nach der Weltmacht* (*Germany's Aims in the First World War*), first published in Germany in 1961, shattered the easy calm within West German historical circles. Its major thesis was that Germany's objectives in July 1914 had undoubtedly been offensive and had been intended to establish Germany's hegemony over continental Europe. The implications of this thesis were profound, for it clearly suggested a similarity between the foreign policy aims of the *Kaiserreich* and the Third Reich, which in turn upheld the idea of a continuity in development between the two regimes. However, it was not only Fischer's message but also his method of delivery which was so significant. His interpretation was based upon an analysis of the interaction between Imperial domestic and foreign policies, and in particular on the role of the traditional elites in German society. Fischer in effect ushered in the start of a methodological revolution in historical research which laid the basis for the emergence of the 'structuralist' school.[6]

Since the late 1960s 'structuralist' historians, such as Broszat and Mommsen, have exerted an enormous influence on our understanding of the Third Reich (although the school has paid even more attention to the *Kaiserreich*). Without resorting to the crudities of historical determinism, they have debunked the notion that Nazism was an 'accident' divorced from Germany's historical development. Instead, they have drawn attention to its continuities with the past: the existence and influence of conservative social elites, especially in the armed forces and the bureaucracy; and the prevalent belief that Germany deserved as of right the status and territory due to a great power. Above all, they have emphasised the complexities of the Third Reich as a power structure by highlighting the limits of Hitler's leadership and forward-planning, and by focusing on the role played by other institutions and social groups in the Third Reich they have underlined the element of continuity provided by Germany's social elites.

However, the 'intentionalists', the conservative opponents of the 'structuralist' interpretation, have continued to maintain a strong rear-guard action. For the likes of Hildebrand and Jäckel Nazism can be directly equated with Hitlerism, and there is no escape from the central importance of Hitler the individual in the Nazi seizure of power and the regime that followed. Even so, it is important to realise that the analysis provided by the 'intentionalists', while considering the personality and ideology of Hitler to be essential, goes well beyond the framework of mere biography. This, in essence, is the stance taken by one of Germany's leading historians, Karl Dietrich Bracher. Bracher upholds the fundamental role of Hitler, and accepts the term Hitlerism as a direct alternative to Nazism. However, as implied by the title of his most famous book, *The German Dictatorship*, published in 1970, he also sees Nazism as a uniquely German/ Austrian phenomenon. It arose in a society shaped by the nineteenth-century 'German problem' and then devastated by war and humiliated by defeat. It succeeded in gaining power because of Hitler's own powerful nationalist ideology and because his policy of legality confused nearly all the opponents of the Nazis until it was too late:

> Hitler's road to power was never inevitable, since rarely in history has there been such a close inter-dependence of general and personal factors and the indispensable role of the individual as in the crucial period between 1919 and 1945, from Hitler's entry into politics to his exit ...
> 5 It was indeed Hitler's *Weltanschauung* and nothing else that mattered in the end, as is seen from the terrible consequences of his racist anti-Semitism in the planned murder of the Jews.[7]

From the early 1980s the historiography of the Third Reich has been further deeply influenced by the growing interest in *Alltagsgeschichte* (the history of everyday life). In many respects this is an outgrowth of the 'structuralist' school, since it attempts to take the historical analysis still further away from the political centre and towards the grass-roots of society. However, this new school of 'social history' has distanced itself from the pioneeering work of the 'structuralists'. Instead, they have tended to identify more closely with the philosophy of the French *Annalistes* whose aims have been to create a more 'total' and more 'human' history. A whole range of studies have now been published which explore the experiences of different social groups in different regions and localities of Germany. They have focused on all sorts of issues: sexual behaviour; the role of women; family structure; and attitudes to death and crime. In so doing they have broadened the methodological basis of historical research by embracing oral history, demographical and anthropological techniques and by exploiting computer technology for quantification. Undoubtedly, such studies have provided new and very different insights into the complexities of the Third Reich.

c) New Perspectives

The unification of Germany in 1989–90 has provided a very new perspective for the study of the Third Reich and for German history in general and historians have not been slow to proffer new insights and observations.

Already by the late 1980s it was being suggested by critics of the *Alltagsgeschichte* approach that by trying to comprehend the behaviour and experiences of ordinary people it was tending to 'normalise' the Third Reich. This has now developed into a more wide-ranging philosophical debate about whether the Third Reich can ever be studied as simply another period of German history or whether it is always going to be seen as a lesson in political morality. For some, like Broszat, it is indeed now time to 'normalise' the Third Reich and to 'historicise' the topic in a proper and normal fashion.[8] In effect, to apply the same rigorous standards of historical research; to move away from the emphasis on the extraordinary politics and ideology of the era and to concentrate instead much more on the patterns of social behaviour which underline vital continuities. For others, such an attitude is not yet thought to be appropriate. The time factor has not yet gone away and the Nazi era is still too close for it to be treated in the same way as the violence of the wars of religion in sixteenth-century Europe. And anyway, it has been argued that in many respects Nazism was a unique regime which should be treated by the historian in a unique way; for alongside the 'normality' of everyday life, there was still created a policy of industrial human annihilation.

From a similar starting-point there has also been the suggestion from the conservative historian Ernst Nolte that there is a need to 'relativise' the Third Reich. He argues that the inhumanity of the Holocaust originated in the class genocide of the Soviets and that the brutality of the Nazi regime must be seen in comparative terms with other regimes such as those of Stalin, Pol Pot and Idi Amin. Moreover, he has argued that Nazism was an understandable reaction to the Bolshevik threat of world revolution and that Hitler's anti-Bolshevism was actually a more fundamental element of his political ideology than anti-Semitism.[9] Nolte's views generated widespread controversy and in the end relatively little real support, for it was thought by many that they amounted to almost an apologia for Nazism, but it emphasised once again how morally 'loaded' is any discussion of this period of German history.

The weight of Germany's Nazi past is also fundamental to the ongoing political controversy about Germany's present national identity. Until 1990 Germany was divided and occupied and it seemed as if the development of a genuine German nation-state had been brought to a catastrophic halt in 1945. Reunification more than anything else acted as a catalyst for Germany to consider its future as a united nation once again whilst also contemplating its past. This has meant that many political issues of the last decade have more often been discussed with an eye to that past. Should Germany's armed forces be allowed to serve outside the country and on what terms? How should the increased number of attacks against immigrant workers be interpreted? Is the restoration of Berlin as the capital merely a recognition of that city's greatness and tradition or does it suggest that Germany is once again looking eastwards and glorifying its Prussian past at the expense of provincial Bonn? And finally what exactly is the role of the New Germany in the evolving European Union – is it to be a partner or a more dominant master?

2 Concluding Thoughts

So where does all this leave the poor history student? First of all it is important to realise that there are no 'correct' conclusions to be drawn from the various debates raised in this volume. All historical writing is essentially a personal and provisional interpretation of the past. However, to be good history it must examine the evidence and provide coherent explanations which are intellectually satisfying and convincing. These are the common objectives shared by academic historians and examination students. Different interpretations are more often than not a result of applying different criteria or focusing on different points of emphasis. This is why it is so important not only to read a variety of history texts, but also to talk through one's ideas with others who are studying the topic. Only then can one begin to feel comfortable with one's own point of view. What follows should be seen in this light. It is merely the interpretation of the present author on several of the key issues. It certainly should not be viewed as definitive. It is presented in the hope that it will form a basis for further discussion.

a) The Third Reich – a Natural Outgrowth of German History?

Few historians would now support the view that German history made Nazism inevitable. However, it would be equally naive to portray it as an 'aberration', divorced from Germany's historical development and alien to the nation. Such an interpretation would make the Nazi retention of power for 12 years almost inexplicable.

It now seems safe to assume that the emergence of the Third Reich can be linked very clearly with several important features of Germany's past. Significantly in the crucial area of foreign affairs it can be seen that the initial thrust of Nazi foreign policy to restore German continental power and to create *Lebensraum* in the east corresponded very closely with the objectives of Imperial Germany at the start of the First World War and actually put into effect by the terms of the Treaty of Brest-Litovsk in 1918. This coincidence of interest helps to explain why the regime enjoyed the backing of the country's conservative elites who had played such an central part in the nation's development since 1871. Rapid industrialisation and urbanisation had created social pressures which the conservative and authoritarian elites were unwilling to defuse by granting political reform until forced to do so by the pressures of military circumstances in 1918. Although these elites were to some extent eclipsed during the Weimar Republic, they were to be revived in 1933 by the alliance with National Socialism. Moreover, despite the increasing radicalisation of the Nazi system that tolerance was never entirely withdrawn. Thus, in the years 1933–45 there was certainly no fundamental social trans-

Postcard by H.V. Norden.

formation and, as a result, essentially the traditional structure of society remained intact.

These points represent important strands of continuity, but they need to be set alongside some fundamental differences between the Third Reich and earlier German history. The *Kaiserreich* did not seek to destroy the federal tradition within Germany: Nazism did. The *Kaiserreich* operated according to a constitution and its values were squarely in the tradition of what Germans call the *Rechtsstaat* (the constitutional state). Citizens enjoyed certain legal rights, which meant, for example, that only civilian courts could curtail an individual's liberty. The Third Reich, despite the 'legal revolution', behaved in a totally arbitrary fashion, which permitted (even encouraged) imprisonment without trial and state violence on a barbaric scale. As for the ideological roots of National Socialism, it is certainly true that most of its political and racial ideas, especially anti-Semitism, pre-dated the Third Reich, but then there is absolutely nothing in Germany's earlier history to suggest the horrors of Auschwitz and all that it represents. The Holocaust is surely on an entirely different scale to any anti-Semitic precedents – it therefore marks a fundamental change rather than merely a difference in degree. Finally, although Nazi foreign policy had common links with imperial ambitions it was founded on an entirely different premise: namely that the Third Reich would create a racist utopia (a 'new order') which would eventually lead to world domination by Germany.

b) Hitler – the Master of the Third Reich?

If one accepts that the establishment of the Third Reich cannot be understood without appreciating its 'roots' in German history whilst also recognising that that the period 1933–45 stands out in sharp relief to both Weimar and the *Kaiserreich,* it is tempting to assume, as trenchant 'intentionalists' would have us believe, that the crucial difference is rooted in the role played by Hitler himself.

Only the most extreme 'structuralist' would now portray Hitler as a mere agent or puppet. Hitler's power was very real, although it was not exerted in the ordered authoritarian fashion projected by the propaganda machine. Hitler's power has been described by Kershaw as that of 'charismatic domination' by which all forms of legal and rational government were undermined by a readiness 'to work towards the Führer'.[10] In other words, Hitler generated an environment in which his followers carried out his presumed intentions. In this way Hitler's personality and ideology led to a dramatic radicalisation of policy in certain key spheres: politically, by the creation of a one-party state brutally upheld by the SS-Police-SD system, which progressively marginalised other sources of power and influence; a reorientation of society by the application of racial laws, followed by a policy of genocide; and finally, in the field of foreign policy, by the drive towards a German (Aryan) world hegemony. It is hard to envisage these developments without Hitler at the helm.

c) The Legacy of the Third Reich

And yet, the house inherited and built by Hitler collapsed under his tutelage. By 1945 Germany as a modern nation-state had in effect ceased to exist. This was the inheritance bequeathed by Hitler's Third Reich and in that sense 1945 was an even greater turning-point than 1933. The Third Reich should be seen as a watershed in German history. Under the malign influence of Hitler, it was able to emerge and then to distort abominably certain tendencies within Germany. However, the Nazi dynamic could not be sustained and the intended new racial world order was never established. Instead, the Third Reich collapsed in an orgy of destruction and Germany thereafter developed along very different lines. If any point in history deserves the title of 'Year Zero' then surely Germany in 1945 has a particularly good claim. Indeed, it is difficult to pin-point anything positive or creative in the legacy of the Third Reich. Perhaps, this is why, even at the start of the twenty-first century, the history of the Third Reich continues to exert such a powerful fascination among both historians and the general public.

References

1   M. Kitchen, *Fascism* (Macmillan, 1976) p. 10
2   Sir R. Vansittart, *Black Record: Germans Past and Present* (1941) p. 2
3   A.J.P. Taylor, *The Course Of German History* (London, 1945) p. 213
4   See W.H. Shirer, *The Rise and Fall of the Third Reich* (London, 1959)
5   See G. Ritter, *Europa und die Deutsche Frage* (Munich, 1948)
6   See F. Fischer, *Germany's Aims in the First World War* (Engl. trans. London, 1966)
7   K.D. Bracher, 'The role of Hitler: Perspectives and Interpretations' in W. Lacquer, (ed) *Fascism* (Penguin, 1979) pp. 200–1
8   M. Broszat in P. Baldwin, (ed) *Reworking the Past* (Boston, 1990) pp. 77–87
9   See E. Nolte, *The European Civil War 1917–45* (Engl. trans. London, 1988)
10 I. Kershaw, *Hitler: Vol 1 Hubris, 1889–1936* (Allen Lane, 1998) pp. 529–31

Summary Diagram
The Third Reich 1933–45

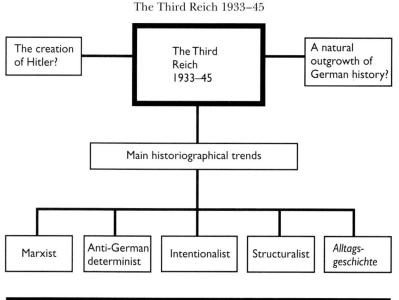

Working on Chapter 9

This chapter has been written with the assumption that students are not only well versed in the history of the Third Reich, but also have a working knowledge of Modern German history in general. Having read all these different views, you may feel at a bit of a loss and not yet ready to tackle these tasks until you are nearing the end of your course and you have gained that broader perspective. However, at some point you will need to confront the big issues, for only then will you begin to appreciate that some of the real 'joys' of history come from assessing cause and consequence or continuity and change. It will not be easy, but it is what real history is all about and it will stand you in very good stead for your examination.

Alternatively, you may already have begun to form your own impressions. But, even then, it is important that you really think through the issues and clarify your thoughts, so that you feel confident of arguing your case in class or in an essay. A good way to achieve this is to examine where you stand on some of the more extreme points of view. Study the following statements:

1. National Socialism was the logical outcome of German history.
2. Nazism was nothing more than Hitlerism.
3. Between 1871 and 1945 there is a clear line of continuity in Germany's history based upon its military and socio-economic structure.
4. The Third Reich was an accident of history.

In the case of each point of view you should do the following:

a) Refer back to your notes made on earlier chapters.
b) Re-read the final section of chapters 2–8 inclusive.
c) Make a list of all the points, ideas and facts to support the statement and all those to counter it.
d) Write a 150 word assessment of the point of view.
e) Compare your assessment with that of a friend. In what ways do you agree and disagree?

Answering essay and structured questions on Chapter 9

Some essay questions are deliberately constructed to test your knowledge and powers of analysis across an extended period of time and/or across topics (synoptic questions). These are some of the most difficult questions you will have to tackle. The Third Reich is very likely to be part of such a focus because of the debates about historical continuity and generic totalitarianism/fascism.
Study the following essay questions:

1 Compare and contrast the regimes of Hitler and Mussolini.
2 Is it accurate to describe both Hitler's Germany and Stalin's Russia as 'totalitarian'?
3 Is it incorrect to define Nazism as Germany's fascism?
4 In what ways did the Third Reich differ from the authoritarian regime of the *Kaiserreich*?

All these essays are 'comparison' questions. Even question 3 falls into this category because it can be answered only by reference to fascism in general. Such questions are not easy. You should tackle them only if you have a good general understanding of all the regimes and periods implied in the question. You also need the ability to organise that knowledge with flexibility and clarity (and if you are in the examination room all this has to be done quite quickly).

How do you tackle such questions? Certainly, you must not write an essay of two halves, because that will prevent effective analysis of the similarities and differences. Instead, it is important that you plan a structure which will encourage comparison throughout. Look at question 1 and complete a matrix such as the one below:

	Hitler's Germany	Mussolini's Italy	Assessment
Ideological principles			
Economic policy			
Social policy			
Structure of regime			
Foreign policy			

As you can see there is a massive amount of material to exploit. It is therefore vital to plan well if you are really going to analyse effectively. By taking a thematic approach you create a clear structure whilst also alluding to the similarities and differences all the time. It will also help you to time yourself effectively. When you have completed a thorough plan, draft a conclusion which tries to make an overall assessment. Now take exactly the same approach with question 4.

Glossary

Anschluss Union of Germany and Austria.
Bekennende Kirche Confessional Church. Protestant churchmen opposed to Nazi interference in the Church.
BDM Bund Deutscher Mädel – League of German Girls.
Blitzkrieg Lightning war. Military strategy to achieve rapid advance by use of motorised infantry, tanks and air-bombardment.
DAF Deutsche Arbeitsfront – German Labour Front. Nazi organisation of workers.
Deutsche Christen German Christians. Protestants who aimed to reconcile Christianity and National Socialism.
DFW Deutsches Frauenwerk – German Women's Enterprise. Nazi women's organisation.
Diktat Right-wing description of Versailles treaty. Literally, a 'dictated' peace.
Einsatzgruppen Action squads. SS units responsible for the murder of inferior racial groups.
Führer Leader.
Führerprinzip The leadership principle.
Gau Region. The basis of Nazi Party organisation.
Gauleiter Regional Party leader.
Gestapo Geheime Staatspolizei – secret state police.
Gleichschaltung Co-ordination. Nazi policy of establishing effective centralised control.
Historikerstreit Historians' dispute. Academic dispute amongst Germany's historians from 1986.
Herrenvolk Master-race.
HJ Hitler Jugend – Hitler Youth.
Junker Prussian landowner.
Kaiser Emperor.
Kaiserreich Imperial Germany 1871–1918.
KDF Kraft durch Freude – Strength through Joy. Nazi organisation for workers' recreation.
Kinder, Küche, Kirche Children, Kitchen, Church. Slogan encouraging women to stay at home.
Kreis District.
Kristallnacht Crystal Night. Pogrom of November 1938.
Kulturkampf Cultural struggle. Bismarck's anti-Catholic policy of the 1870s.
Landtag Provincial parliament.
Lebensborn Literally 'Spring of Life'. Nazi organisation to care for unmarried (Aryan) mothers.
Lebensraum Living-space. Policy of expansion.
Luftwaffe Air-force.
Mein Kampf *My Struggle*. Hitler's autobiography and political exposition (1924).

Mit Brennender Sorge *With Burning Concern.* Papal encyclical of 1937 critical of Nazism.

Mittelstand Middle class. Traditionally referred to the artisan/shopkeeper rather than the new industrial entrepreneur.

Napolas Elite schools.

NSDAP Nationalsozialistische Deutsche Arbeiterpartei – National Socialist German Workers' Party.

NSF Nationalsozialistische Frauenschaft – National Socialist Womanhood.

NSLB Nationalsozialistische Lehrer Bund – National Socialist Teachers' League.

OKW Oberkommando der Wehrmacht – High Command of the Armed Forces. Created in 1938 to bring forces under Hitler's control.

Ordensburgen Elite schools.

Putsch Coup or revolt.

Rechtsstaat Constitutional state. State based upon the rule of law.

Reich Empire.

Reichsrat Second chamber of German parliament, representing federal provinces.

Reichstag Representative chamber of parliament.

Reichsstatthalter Reich Commissioners. Appointed in 1933 to oversee Nazi take-over of federal provinces.

SA Sturm Abteilung – Stormtroopers.

SS Schutz Staffeln – Protection squad.

Stahlhelm Steel Helmet. Para-military organisation of veterans. Right-wing.

Stufenplan Gradual plan. Theory that Hitler's foreign policy was set to follow a number of stages.

Volk A people/nation with ethnic and cultural identities.

Völkischer Beobachter *People's Observer.* Nazi newspaper.

Volksgemeinschaft People's community. Nazi concept of national integration based upon race.

Wehrwirtschaft Defence economy. Theory that the German economy should be geared in peacetime to the needs of war.

Further Reading

Textbooks

Because of the importance of this topic in German and European history it would be worthwhile looking at several general textbooks. You should not make detailed notes on them, but you should try to understand how the author sees the Third Reich in the broader context. By far the most accessible of the many general histories of Germany is:

William Carr, *A History of Germany 1815–1990* (Edward Arnold 4th ed., 1992)

This is a thorough but readable survey, which highlights the differing historical interpretations.

More intellectually demanding are:

Volker Berghahn, *Modern Germany* (CUP 2nd ed., 1987)
Gordon Craig, *Germany 1866–1945* (OUP, 1981)

The emphasis and approach of the two books is entirely different. It would be a good idea to see if you can detect these differences by dipping into one or two of the relevant chapters of each book.

Biographies

There are numerous biographies of Hitler, though many are sensationalist and populist in style. The very first major academic biography, published as long ago as 1952, has stood the the test of time very well. This is:

Alan Bullock, *Hitler. A Study in Tyranny* (Penguin, 1962)

This book remains a historical classic. It is an excellent example of how good academic history can be written in an easy-going style. In particular, read chapters 3–5, which consider the rise to power and the creation of the dictatorship, and chapter 7, which shows how a good biographer actually gets inside the mind of his subject.

However, it is now being superseded by:

Ian Kershaw, *Hitler: Vol 1 Hubris, 1889–1936* (Vol. 2 pending) (Allen Lane 1998)

For a long time academic historians tended to fight shy of the biographical approach because they were only too aware of its inadequacies in explaining the Third Reich as a whole. This book, written by one of Britain's leading experts on Nazi Germany, is a real *tour de force*, which tries to provide a genuine synthesis between the structuralist and biographical approaches.

However, if the 845 pages of Volume 1 seem somewhat daunting, then refer to:

Ian Kershaw, *Hitler* (Longman, 1991)

Another brief biographical survey well worth dipping into is:

David Welch, *Hitler* (UCL Press, 1998)

And for other other leading Nazis the best place to start is:

Joachim Fest, *The Face of the Third Reich* (Penguin, 1977)

Historiographical Reviews

By far the best general survey of the controversies surrounding Nazi Germany is:
Ian Kershaw, *The Nazi Dictatorship. Problems and Perspectives of Interpretation* (Edward Arnold 3rd ed., 1993)
However, although it is well-organised, so that each chapter considers a separate area of controversy, it is not an easy read and you will have to take it slowly and think critically about the ideas raised. If you can persevere, you will be well rewarded.
Alternatively, a masterly synthesis of the key issues is provided by:
R. Geary, *Hitler and Nazism* (Routledge, 1993)

Specialist Studies

If you wish to study some of the historical controversies more deeply you will need to select your reading with great care. The academic literature on the Third Reich is enormous and much of it is detailed and very specialised. The following are suggested 'starting-points' for various aspects of the topic:

a) Rise to Power
Peter D. Stachura (ed.), *The Nazi Machtergreifung* (London, 1983)
W.S. Allen, *The Nazi Seizure of Power: The Experience of a Single Town* (Eyre & Spottiswoode, 1966)
Ian Kershaw (ed.), *Why did German Democracy Fail?* (1990)

b) Structure of the Regime
Karl Dietrich Bracher, *The German Dictatorship* (Penguin, 1973)

c) Society and Economy
R. Grunberger, *A Social History of the Third Reich* (Penguin, 1974)
R. Overy, *The Nazi Economic Recovery 1932–1938* (2nd ed. London 1996)
R. Bessel (ed.), *Life in the Third Reich* (Oxford, 1987)

d) Foreign Policy
William Carr, *Arms, Autarky and Aggression* (London 2nd ed., 1979)
Klaus Hildebrand, *The Third Reich* (Allen & Unwin, 1984)

Sources

For the definitive collection of documents in English refer to:
J. Noakes & G. Pridham (ed.), *Nazism 1919–1945* 4 Vols. (Exeter, 1983–1998)
For a more select collection of sources and also a range of pictorial material look at:
J. Laver *Nazi Germany 1933–1945* (Hodder & Stoughton, 1991)

Index